The Learning Work

Gary Paulsen

by Stephanie True Peters

The Learning Works, Inc.
Santa Barbara, California

The Learning Works

Editing and page design by
Kimberley Clark
Cover photo by
Ruth Wright Paulsen

❧

Grateful acknowledgment is given to Jennifer Flannery and to Gary M. Salver, for his book *Presenting Gary Paulsen.*

This book is dedicated to Dan, who told me to test my wings, and to Jackson, who I hope will love to read as we do.

The Learning Works, Inc.
P. O. Box 6187
Santa Barbara, CA 93160

Copyright © 1999—The Learning Works, Inc.
All rights reserved.

Library of Congress Cataloging-in-Publication Data:

```
Peters, Stephanie True, 1965-
   Gary Paulsen / by Stephanie True Peters.
      p.    cm. -- (The Learning Works meet the author series)
   Summary: Describes the multifaceted life of author Gary Paulsen,
whose writings include adventure stories, survival tales, historical
novels, sports stories, and nature books.
   ISBN 0-88160-324-4 (pbk.)
   1. Paulsen, Gary--Juvenile literature.  2. Authors, American--20th
century--Biography--Juvenile literature.  3. Young adult fiction-
-Authorship--Juvenile literature.   [1. Paulsen, Gary.  2. Authors,
American.]   I. Title.   II. Series.
PS3566.A834Z83   1999
813'.54--dc21
[B]
                                                           98-54725
                                                                CIP
                                                                 AC
```

Contents

Gary Paulsen with Sheba, one of his sled dogs

Preface

*My own self I couldn't believe how much there was to learn.
Thought just in living I'd learned such a load my head couldn't
hold it all. . . . But when I got inside the books she brought me.
Oh my, oh my Lord.*

Sarny: A Life Remembered

The Minnesota night air was cold on Gary Paulsen's
skin. The fourteen-year-old was heading to the local bar
again, hoping to sell some newspapers to the drunk men
for twice what they cost. It was something he did from time
to time, to earn money and to get out of the house.

"House" was how he thought of the apartment he lived
in. Not "home." A home meant parents who paid attention to their children, who didn't drink themselves drunk
nearly every day. For Gary, trudging through the cold was
better than being with his parents.

The wind seemed to sneak through his overcoat no matter how tightly he held it closed, and the bar was still a block away. So when he passed the library and saw that the light was on, he decided to make a detour and go inside, just to get warm.

Once inside, Gary walked cautiously into the main room. He spotted a few people sitting in chairs, reading. But they didn't pay any attention to him, so he turned away.

"May I help you?"

Gary turned back, startled at the sudden voice. A tall, thin woman with glasses and white hair had appeared behind the library desk.

"May I help you?" she asked again.

Gary shifted uneasily. "It's cold outside," he mumbled. "I just came in to get warm."

The librarian studied him for a moment. "Well, since you're here," she said, "would you like a library card?"

Gary blinked. "A library card?" he repeated.

The librarian nodded. "Come over here and tell me your name so I can fill out a card for you."

A minute later, Gary was holding his first library card—the first official document he'd ever had with his name on it. He examined it, then started to slide it into his pocket.

"Would you like a book?"

That question took the boy by surprise. Few people in his life had ever given him anything. Now here was a woman he'd never met before offering him a book.

But he wasn't about to let on that that was anything special. He gave a half-shrug and replied, "Sure," in a cocky tone, as if he didn't really care one way or the other.

The librarian pushed a thin volume across the desk to him.

"When you're finished with that one, you bring it back and I'll give you another. Okay?"

Gary shrugged again. Then he picked up the book, gathered his coat close around him, and disappeared out the door.

He didn't go to the bar that night. Instead, he hurried back to the apartment building. But he didn't go upstairs to where his mother and father were. He headed for his sanctuary, the basement.

In the basement, near the furnace, he had set up an old easy chair beneath a bare light bulb. He had a stash of crackers and peanut butter from the kitchen to snack on. When things in the apartment got bad, as they did many nights, he escaped to the easy chair.

He carried his book to the chair and dug out some crackers. With the warmth from the furnace washing over him, he settled in. But he didn't open the book right away.

He pulled the library card from his pocket and studied it again. With a finger, he touched the name the librarian had written down—his name. Gary Paulsen.

It would take him more than a month to read the book the librarian had given him. But from that moment on, books were a part of his life.

After the first volume, he read another. That took him two weeks. But the pace picked up soon after, until he was reading nearly two books a week. Westerns, science fiction, and even the occasional classic like *Moby Dick*— Gary read them all, and through his reading he escaped from the difficulties of everyday life.

But reading was more than an escape. He learned from

books, learned that there was more in the world than what his life so far had taught him. That was a lesson he never forgot.

Gary Paulsen went on to write his own books—more than 130, in fact—adventure stories, survival tales, historical novels, nonfiction, sports books, nature books. Many of the plots and characters developed in his fictional works are drawn from experiences he had growing up. The nonfiction titles he writes also highlight details from his life.

And what a life it has been! Gary Paulsen has been a farmworker, a soldier, a sailor, a trapper, and a rancher. He has worked for a carnival, in construction, and for aerospace companies. He's lived in Minnesota, California, Illinois, the Philippines, Texas, Colorado, and New Mexico. He's sailed the seas in boats he fixed up, ridden a motorcycle cross-country, and driven dogsled teams through the wilds of Alaska and Minnesota. These are the experiences that have found life again in the pages of Gary Paulsen's books.

Chapter One
Believing

*It was him for that Christmas and all the Christmases since;
it was him later when Matthew did not come home again and I
went to the funeral and tried to tell Mother he was just sleeping
and not to cry; it was him when Father did come home from
Europe and we had Christmases together; it was him for each and
every Christmas of each and every year that I have lived since
then, and will still be him for each and every Christmas of each
and every year that I have yet remaining.*

It was him.

A Christmas Sonata

Eunice Paulsen held her infant son Gary tightly as she
kissed her husband good-bye. Oscar Paulsen was an officer
in the army. The year was 1939, and though the United
States wasn't to enter World War II for another two years,
Oscar was on his way to Europe to join General George
Patton's staff. Gary and his mother wouldn't see him again
for seven years.

Eunice and Gary moved into an apartment in Minneapolis, Minnesota. Checks from Gary's father arrived regularly, but money was still tight. Eunice was a strong woman, though, and determined to make a home, however poor, for her child.

One night, when Gary was four, he called out weakly to his mother.

"What is it, punkin?" she replied.

"I don't feel good," Gary whimpered.

This was nothing new; Gary had a lot of respiratory problems as an infant and even had pneumonia in the past year. Eunice kept careful watch over him that night, and when his illness grew worse instead of better, she hurried him to the doctor. The doctor confirmed her suspicions: Gary had pneumonia again. He was admitted to the hospital.

Eunice visited him constantly, trying to comfort him through the oxygen tent he was kept in. Though she was worried, she was sure Gary would recover as he had the previous times. It was unthinkable that he wouldn't.

The doctors, however, weren't so sure Gary would pull through. In fact, there came a day when they thought they had done everything they could for him—everything but let him die in peace. Without telling Eunice, they called in a priest to give Gary last rites.

Eunice was with Gary when the priest arrived. At the sound of footsteps, she turned from her son to see who was behind her. Her expression changed from one of tenderness for her son to absolute fury at the sight of the priest. A priest in a hospital meant only one thing: death. She knew the doctors wouldn't have called for him unless they were convinced Gary was going to die. But she refused to allow that to happen.

With an enraged yell, she forced the priest away from Gary's bedside.

"Not now, get out of here!" she shouted again and again. "He's not going to die!"

Gary saw and heard it all, and he believed her when she said he wouldn't die. The fury in her voice and in her eyes made him think of a tiger protecting its young. It was an image he would never forget.

As his mother predicted, Gary recovered, and their lives continued. Eunice worked in a laundry to help their financial situation, leaving Gary in the care of neighbors in the apartment building. Most of the people tolerated him with patience, giving him cookies and letting him listen to the radio and play war.

However, one surly old man who lived in the building made it clear he didn't like children—especially Gary. Gary avoided him as much as possible. But one day a few weeks before Christmas, Gary was hurrying past the man's apartment when he saw a sight that stopped him in his tracks.

The old man was standing in his kitchen. He was wearing a red suit with white trim and a black belt. On his feet were big black boots and on his head was a red hat with a white pompon at the end. Behind him, his wife was holding a white beard.

Gary stared in disbelief, and before he could stop himself he asked, "Are you Santa Claus?"

The old man rasped a nasty laugh. "Yeah, I'm Santa Claus," he replied.

For weeks, four-year-old Gary had been dreaming about Santa Claus. Suddenly, Santa Claus was there— and he was the man Gary most feared.

Gary's world came crashing down. He ran from the open door to his own apartment and cried. When Eunice found out what had happened, she got a bit of the tiger look in her eye again. Perhaps it was this chance meeting or a desire to be with family at Christmas that prompted Eunice's announcement two days later.

"We're going to spend the holidays with your aunt and uncle in northern Minnesota. You'll get to see your cousin Raleigh. Won't that be fun?"

Raleigh was a few years older than Gary and bedridden because of a kidney ailment. Gary wasn't so sure it was going to be much fun being with Raleigh and his family, but he knew better than to argue with his mother. Besides, since Santa Claus was his mean old neighbor, it didn't really matter where they spent Christmas.

They arrived in northern Minnesota after a two-day train trip. His uncle and aunt ran a small store on the edge of a lake and lived in rooms that adjoined it. Gary held back from his relatives at first, especially Raleigh. But he soon got over the strangeness of playing with a cousin who couldn't get out of bed.

Raleigh's attitude helped that some. When he wasn't under the influence of the medicine that made him fall asleep, Raleigh insisted that Gary report on everything that was happening in his father's store. Like all boys of that era, Raleigh and Gary were consumed by the images of the war. Gary was a "scout" and the customers were "the enemy."

Eunice's attitude helped Gary relax, too. She laughed so hard with her sister, Gary's aunt, that sometimes she had to hold onto the counter. The tightness that was around her eyes at home disappeared.

And then there was the wonderful Christmas tree. It had lights and decorations and an angel on top. The tree almost made up for the fact that Santa Claus was that mean old man back home.

When Gary told Raleigh about the old man, Raleigh snorted. "There isn't any Santa Claus at all," he informed Gary.

Now Gary didn't know what to believe. Could his cousin be right? And if he was, was no Santa Claus better than a mean old man Santa Claus? The questions pinballed around in Gary's mind all Christmas Eve.

Then something happened that night that made everything right again. Raleigh had been carried from his bed to the living room to enjoy the tree with the family. Suddenly, Gary's uncle shushed everyone.

"What's that noise?" he said, looking from one boy to the other.

Gary was about to say he didn't hear anything when he heard it. Sleigh bells!

Everyone hurried through the store to the front door. There in front of them appeared one, two, three, four reindeer—and they were pulling a sleigh! Propped on the seat was a big bag of presents. Beside the bag sat a bearded man in a red suit. Gary knew at a glance he wasn't the mean old man from Minneapolis. But was it Santa?

At Raleigh's urging and his mother's nod, Gary stepped outside. Hesitantly, he touched one of the reindeer. It swung its head around and gazed at him with liquid brown eyes. Then Gary crunched through the snow to the man in the sleigh. He climbed into the sleigh and, with a backward glance at Raleigh, tugged gently at the man's beard. It didn't move.

The mean old man from back home vanished from Gary's mind forever. *This* was Santa Claus, right here in front of him. Gary knew it, and when he hurried back to Raleigh's side, he knew Raleigh knew it, too.

When Christmas was over, Gary and his mother returned to their Minneapolis apartment. Raleigh died a few months later, so Gary never saw him again. But he never forgot the look of belief that he saw reflected in his cousin's eyes that Christmas Eve.

Chapter Two
Grandmother

"I'm here," she repeated. "I'll always be here."
She rubbed his forehead and cheeks with the back of her hand,
a gentle touch, then used her fingers to straighten his mussed hair.
She had her hair back in a bun, gray and black mixed in a thick
coiled braid. But some hairs had come loose and he saw that she had
flour on her cheeks.

The Cookcamp

In 1944, Gary and his mother moved from Minneapolis to Chicago, Illinois. Eunice took a job working in a munitions factory and hired an elderly woman named Clara to stay with Gary.

Clara was not much of a caretaker. She seemed to pay more attention to the radio than she did to Gary. Day-to-day life wasn't very happy for Gary. He was lonely for his mother and looked forward to her return each night. Together they would sit at the kitchen table and she would tell him about the factory while he munched on a candy bar or examined an empty shell casing she had brought him.

Then those cozy nighttime visits changed.

One night Gary was awakened by the sound of his mother's crying. He padded into the kitchen and found her with her head down on the table. In front of her was his father's picture and a letter. The letter, it turned out, was from his father.

When his mother saw Gary, she beckoned him to her. She held him close and cried hard for a long time. Then she tried to explain.

"Daddy says he has a . . . friend . . . in France," she said.

Gary didn't understand. "But isn't that good? I bet the soldiers need friends when they fight the enemy," he said.

His mother didn't answer, and it was only much later that Gary understood that his father's friend was a woman.

Soon after receiving the letter, Eunice started going to bars. She usually took Gary with her. He had learned a lot of songs from listening to the radio with Clara. He sang them while standing on the bar and the customers gave him money which he used to buy chicken dinners and soda. After he ate, he would sit down and wait for his mother to decide it was time to go home.

His mother was a very attractive woman. Her striking blonde hair and shapely figure reminded him of a movie star at times. He knew other people thought she was pretty, too. He had seen how men reacted when they saw his mother. They stood as close to her as they could. In the bars, they bought her beer and other drinks until she was laughing and dancing and acting silly-happy.

Gary hated his mother when she was like that. But scrunched up on the bench in their booth, Gary was powerless to stop the men or his mother.

One evening, a large man named Casey danced with his mother again and again. He came home with Gary and his mother and stayed over that night. A week later his mother told Gary that Casey was coming to live with them. Gary was to call him "Uncle."

Gary despised him. "Uncle" Casey was not his uncle, and though he tried hard to win Gary over with candy and other presents, Gary refused to bend. He didn't know why his mother wanted to spend time with Uncle Casey.

Eunice tried to explain. "I'm lonely, punkin, so lonely without your father," she said. "Try to understand."

But when it became clear that Gary didn't or wouldn't try to understand, Eunice made a decision.

"You're going to visit your grandmother for the summer," she told him one day. "She lives way up north and cooks meals for men who are building a new road. You'll like it up there with her." She smiled hopefully.

A few days later Gary was at the train depot, ready to take his first train ride by himself. His mother pinned a note to his jacket, gave him a kiss, and handed him into the care of a porter.

The porter led him to a seat. "How old are you, son?" the man asked kindly.

"Five," Gary replied in a small voice.

"Well, don't you worry about a thing. We'll take good care of you."

Gary relaxed a little and turned to look out the window. Before too long, he had fallen asleep.

The miles and hours passed by. Day turned to night, night turned to day, until at last the porter told Gary they had arrived at his stop.

At first Gary thought he was joking. The depot stood alone in the midst of huge trees. How could this be where his grandmother lived? There weren't even any houses anywhere!

The man at the depot seemed to think there had been a mistake, too.

"He's looking for his grandmother?" he repeated, giving Gary a long look. "Well, she hasn't been here looking for him. Are you sure this is where he's supposed to be?"

The porter shrugged. "That's what his ticket says."

So Gary and his suitcase got off the train to wait at the depot. And wait. And wait. It seemed like hours.

At last, a huge dump truck roared up to the depot and a woman got out of the passenger side. She smiled when she saw Gary.

"Bet you thought we'd forgotten you, didn't you?" she said, holding her arms open wide.

All of Gary's emotions—exhaustion from the ride, anxiety at not knowing where his grandmother was, loneliness from missing his mother—came bubbling to the surface. He ran into his grandmother's arms and cried.

On the truck ride back to the work camp, exhaustion won out over the other emotions. Gary fell asleep wedged between his grandmother and the truck driver.

He half-awoke when the truck pulled into the work camp. His grandmother ushered him into the cook trailer, the place he would call home for the summer. She tucked him into a cot back behind the kitchen area. Gary fell sound asleep, too wrung out from the trip to care about anything but the pillow under his head and the warm blanket snuggled over him.

The next morning, Gary was ready to face his new surroundings. He was timid around his grandmother at first. But soon he was too busy to think about being bashful. While she made stacks and stacks of pancakes and pan after pan of hot buttery biscuits, his grandmother told him how to set the big tables for breakfast.

Just as he was putting the last coffee cup in place, the workmen came in to eat. To five-year-old Gary's eyes, these were the biggest men he'd ever seen in his life. Their arms were thick and muscular, their faces were broad and sunburned, and their powerful legs seemed like tree trunks. Gary shrank back, shy again in their overwhelming presence.

His grandmother coaxed him out of his shyness.

"Here, bring these biscuits over to that table," she whispered, handing him a plate piled high. One of the men took the plate from him, ruffled his hair, and smiled. Each time Gary brought more food, he got the same reaction. The men were enormous, like bears, but gentle and polite. Gary couldn't help but relax.

After a few days, Gary had learned his grandmother's mealtime routine. She was up at dawn to make breakfast and set the table. Then she served the men, cleaned up, and began again for lunch. Meat and potatoes, gravy and biscuits, and pie with milk and coffee—the huge men devoured everything. When lunch was done, it was time to start getting supper ready.

Gary helped out any way he could. When he had some

free time, he sat on the front step, watching a little chipmunk that came looking for crumbs, trying to get it to eat from his hand. He explored the woods surrounding the trailer. In the distance, he could hear the roar of the truck motors, the crash of trees falling, and the boom of gravel loads being dumped.

His days were busy, but not terribly exciting. He longed to see how those interesting sounds were made. Then one day he got his wish.

The men usually played cards after dinner. When his grandmother learned that Gary didn't understand the game, she asked one of the men to show him how it was played.

"Help me win a few hands, boy," the man said, gesturing for Gary to sit in his lap. Gary obeyed and tried to follow the game. But he was tired from the day's work, and dozed off. When the card game was through, the man carried Gary, still half-asleep, to his cot.

"I'm taking him with me tomorrow," Gary heard the man whisper to his grandmother. "He needs to do some work outdoors to get a little meat on his bones."

In the morning, Gary helped out with breakfast like he always did. But he kept a careful eye on the man from the night before. Would he remember what he'd said?

Breakfast ended, and as usual the workers headed out the door. Gary was crestfallen. The man had forgotten!

Then the man turned around. "Well, are you coming to help me today, or aren't you?" he asked, with a twinkle in his eye.

Gary flew to the door. The man scooped him up and carried him through the woods to a huge gravel pile. At the base of the pile was a tractor.

"It's my job to push that gravel into the dump trucks so they can haul it to the new road," the man explained. "Think you can help me do that?" Gary nodded, too excited to speak.

Moments later, they were high up inside the cab of the tractor. The man pulled a few levers and pushed a few buttons and the engine roared to life. The noise was deafening and Gary screamed, half with fright, half with delight.

From that day on, Gary rode with one or another of the men. One day he'd be with the dump trucks, the next with the road grader, until he had ridden with practically every worker. They seemed to fight over who would get the honor of having him in their truck. He ate his meals with the men, too. Though he was still scrawny compared to them, he felt like a man when he was with them.

But underneath all the wonderful things—the beauty of the forest, the feather-light feel of the chipmunk taking food from his hand, the roar of the trucks, the warmth of his grandmother's touch—Gary missed his mother. Some days his homesickness was so strong it made him ache.

Gary had told his grandmother about Uncle Casey. He knew that she was writing to his mother constantly, imploring and admonishing her by turns to remember she was a married woman and that the war would be over one day. Finally, Eunice wrote to Gary.

"I miss you very much," the letter read. "I'm sending money for a train ticket so you can come home."

That night, Gary's grandmother seemed sad. She told him stories of when she was a little girl growing up in Norway, then a young girl coming to America. She told him about his grandfather, her husband, who had died a long time ago. She described their farm in northern Minnesota. On and on into the night she talked and Gary listened, learning about his heritage.

Two days later, after a whirlwind of packing and good-byes, Gary climbed into a truck, rode to the depot, and boarded a train that took him back to Chicago.

Eunice was waiting for him. She folded him into her arms and hugged him tightly.

"I missed you," she whispered, half-laughing and half-crying.

"Me, too," said Gary. And he had, but suddenly he realized he was missing his grandmother almost as much as he had missed his mother. The memories of the summer flooded over him until he had to let them out.

"I want to tell you about the trucks, and the chipmunk, and the trees," Gary said.

His mother ruffled his hair just as the men had, only lighter. "Tell me," she said. "We have lots of time together now. Just you and me."

Chapter Three
The Voyage to Father

The water detonated, surged up at his face, and a shark's gaping maw, teeth flashing in the moonlight, triangular-death-razor-sharp teeth, blew up and out of the darkness, slashed past his face in a ripping sideways motion, and savagely raked down the side of the hull, slamming against the side of the boat so hard it knocked the Frog sideways.

The Voyage of the Frog

The ship plowed through the ocean waves of the Pacific. It was so large that the deck beneath Gary's feet was as stable as a floor. The bow pointed toward the sun, which was just peeking over the horizon, moments from filling the new day with its bright heat. To the stern, the sky was still dark, not yet touched by the early rays.

If Gary had been older than his seven years, he might have thought about how the light ahead and dark behind mimicked his life just now. In front of him lay the promise of a bright beginning. Behind him were some dark memories he was happy to escape.

Gary and his mother were on board a navy ship headed for the Philippines. The year was 1945 and the Second World War had just ended. Gary's father, an army sergeant, had been stationed in the Philippines helping the island chain rebuild after the devastation caused by the war. Gary was excited to be on his way to his father, even though he only knew him as a black and white picture on the wall of their dingy Chicago apartment.

Chicago. Had it really been less than a month since he and his mother had left that city behind? He vividly recalled the moment his mother had opened the letter from his father. The war had just ended and both Gary and his mother had been eagerly anticipating Oscar's return. This letter, they hoped, would hold the details of that important event.

She read the letter out loud, her eyes scanning the page rapidly. She smiled when she came to the part about being reunited with her husband. But the smile turned to a slight frown a moment later.

Gary's father wasn't coming to them. Instead, they were to hurry to San Francisco to board a ship that would take them to the Philippines where Oscar was now stationed. The ship left in two weeks. If they missed it, they might not get on another for a long time.

Gary and his mother would have to take a train from Chicago to San Francisco. The trip could take a few days if all went smoothly—longer if it didn't.

It didn't. They made it by train as far as Minneapolis. When they reached the train depot, they were told that seating was being given to soldiers first, civilians second. And there were soldiers everywhere.

Eunice was frantic. If they couldn't get to San Francisco, they wouldn't make it onto the ship. Who knew when another ship might be able to take them to the Philippines?

Again and again she approached the ticket window, only to be turned away. Then a young soldier tapped her on the shoulder.

"Excuse me, ma'am," he said, "but I couldn't help but overhear you. My buddy and I are trying to get to San Francisco quickly, too. If we purchased a car, would you be willing to split the driving with us?"

Gary's mother hesitated. She desperately wanted to get to San Francisco, but these men were strangers. Finally, though, she decided she had to take the soldiers up on their offer. Hours later, Gary, his mother, and the two soldiers were driving across the country.

At first, Gary enjoyed the ride. But soon, it became tedious. They had two thousand miles to cover quickly, so pit stops for eating and going to the bathroom were few and far between.

They traveled mile after mile of flat, dusty road. His mother sat up front with the soldier who had bought the car. Gary was stuffed in back with the luggage and the other soldier, a silent, sullen man who was missing a hand.

Gary longed to ask the soldier how he had lost his hand. In the past years, he had listened to countless radio programs, seen newspaper headlines and movie clips, and overheard conversations about America's enemies. Such media coverage had made the war look and sound clean and heroic, almost glamorous. Here was a man who had been there, actually faced the enemy in mortal combat.

But when he finally gathered up the courage to ask the soldier about his injury, his mother snapped at him to leave the man alone. She needn't have bothered, though, for the soldier barely noticed that Gary had spoken.

With the dull landscape out the window and the tight-lipped man beside him, Gary settled into the boredom of the road trip.

Gary had been feeling slightly carsick for much of the ride—brought on by the combination of constant move-ment, greasy roadside food, and hot dusty air—but sud-denly he felt a lot worse. He was feverish and threw up several times. Spots began to appear on his body.

Two days later, after they finally reached San Fran-cisco, a military doctor confirmed what Eunice suspected. Gary had chicken pox!

The timing was terrible. The doctor's duty was to give everybody boarding the ship a physical to ensure they were healthy enough to make the trip and were free of infectious disease. As chicken pox is an infectious disease, the long drive from Minneapolis would be for nothing.

The doctor took pity on them. "I'll pass him," he said, signing off on a form. "But the one you really have to convince is the captain. Without his okay, the boy won't be allowed on board."

Gary's mother was silent, then nodded. She thanked the doctor, and hurried to the hotel where she and Gary were staying. She tucked Gary into bed, asked a woman down the hall to keep an eye on him, then left in search of the captain.

That night, Eunice woke him up around midnight. She was with a stranger, a man he soon learned was the captain.

"Don't bother getting dressed; we have to hurry," his mother said. And hurry they did—from the hotel to a taxi to the ship where Gary was rolled into a blanket and sneaked on board.

He was unrolled into a brilliant white cabin below deck. It was a small room with two bunks and a bathroom, or "head" as he learned to call it in navy lingo. He spent the next nine days in confinement in that room, waiting for his spots to clear up. His mother visited once a day, but his only other companion was a sailor named Harding, the ship's medic.

Finally, though, Gary was allowed on deck. Once his eyes became accustomed to the bright sunlight reflected off the sea, he looked around him, trying to see everything at once.

Moments later, he would see something he would forever wish he hadn't seen.

A plane in trouble was circling overhead, attempting an emergency landing. As its engines faltered, it crashed, skipped across the water, and smashed into the waves again. It was the beginning of a nightmare. As Gary watched, the wounded passengers, mostly women and children, struggled out of the wrecked plane only to fall into the water. Rescue boats from the ship were already on their way to them, but they weren't fast enough. The sharks were faster.

Gary watched, unable to look away though he desperately wanted to, as the sharks attacked the people again and again. The boats were only able to rescue a few of the survivors.

The next eighteen hours were filled with blood, screams, and death, as Gary's mother worked side by side with Harding to tend to the survivors' wounds and ease their suffering. Gary, unseen by the adults, witnessed it all.

In the days that followed that horrible experience, Gary tried to erase the memories by exploring the ship from top to bottom. Several sailors, rough men with crude ways, were friendly to him, though Gary soon realized they were only using him to get to know his mother. Still, their friendship was better than nothing, and Gary held on to the hope that once he and his mother were reunited with his father, all the other men would go away forever.

Finally, after weeks of travel on the open seas, Gary and Eunice were called on deck to watch as the huge ship slowly docked into the port of Manila. It was late in the fall of 1945. Back home in Chicago, the weather was cold and snowy. Here in the Philippines, in the middle of the Pacific Ocean, it was warm and tropical.

When the ship was safely tied off, Gary and Eunice went in search of Oscar, Gary's father. Gary scanned the crowd of Filipinos, hoping to spot the face that matched the black and white photograph of his father.

But his father wasn't there. Instead, a broad-shouldered man with a hard look in his eyes and a submachine gun in his hands approached them. He introduced himself as Sergeant Ryland, loaded their luggage into a jeep, and drove them away from the dock toward their new home.

As the jeep bumped through the war-torn streets of Manila, Gary listened to snatches of conversation between Ryland and his mother. He could tell that his mother didn't like Sergeant Ryland. She was the wife of Ryland's commanding officer. She knew she deserved to be treated with respect, but Ryland's manner was sarcastic and insolent.

When Eunice commented on the number of craters in the street, Ryland rolled his eyes. "There was a war here."

Eunice's back got very stiff and when she spoke, her voice was tight.

"I know there was a war here. I know about the war."

Ryland snorted. "Yeah, I'll bet you had it real bad stateside, didn't you? Did you have to go without sugar once or twice?"

Eunice said very little the rest of the ride. But when they reached the village of houses where they were to live, she couldn't keep silent.

"Where are the walls?" she said, staring at the houses with dismay. "Everything's all open. You can see right through them!"

Gary, on the other hand, thought the houses were interesting. They stood on stilts and there were walls, of a sort—woven bamboo matting four feet high topped with screens. They all looked identical to Gary, but Ryland had no trouble picking out their house. He stopped the jeep in front of number twenty-six.

For the next two-and-a-half years, number twenty-six would be Gary's home.

Chapter Four
Life in the Philippines

"This year we're going to have a real Christmas," Mother said in my room one day. "We're going to do it right and be a family."
Her voice was soft, but her eyes had that hard edge they got when she became angry. "There's been too much of this other business, hasn't there? Too much of running around and playing cards..."
And drinking, I thought, but I didn't say anything.

Eastern Sun, Winter Moon:
An Autobiographical Odyssey

"Aaaah!"

Eunice's shriek brought Gary running from his new bedroom. He found his mother in the living room, staring at the ceiling in disgust.

"Lizards!" she spat. "They're everywhere! Get me the broom, quick, and help me kill them."

Gary did as he was told. When he returned with the broom, he looked at the lizards with fascination. They had only been in Manila a few hours, but already the seven-year-old had seen and heard stranger things than he ever had in Chicago or Minnesota.

Like the pet monkey, Harold, kept by the people next door. Harold wasn't a nice monkey, though; the woman had warned Gary that if he got too close, Harold would bite him or throw dirt and rocks at him. Gary made a vow to himself to steer clear of Harold.

Then there was the barbed-wire fence which surrounded the village, and the towers which Ryland said held men with machine guns. "For your protection," was the only explanation Ryland gave for the towers and the fences.

And now lizards. As Gary stood back and watched, his mother thrashed at them again and again. Any she hit fell to the floor, but quickly ran to the wall and back up to the ceiling again. One or two landed in her hair, sending her flying to the kitchen sink to pull them out. It might have gone on like that all afternoon, but suddenly a strong voice stopped both Eunice and Gary in their tracks.

"What do you think you're doing?"

Gary stared at the man in the doorway. He knew who it was right away. He recognized him from the black and white photo.

Oscar Paulsen was an imposing figure. He had his uniform khakis on, his hat in his hand. He had black hair and brown eyes, so different from Gary's blond hair and blue eyes. He was smiling.

Gary had dreamed of this moment, of meeting his father, for so long. But he couldn't make his feet move. He was too overwhelmed, paralyzed with shyness.

Eunice seemed taken aback for a moment, too. She put a hand to her tangled hair and to her dusty face in a vain attempt to make herself tidier. Then she laughed helplessly and said, "Oh darling, I wanted to look nice for you after so long."

Oscar didn't seem to care. He folded her into his arms and kissed her. When they broke apart, Oscar turned his attention to his son.

"Well, then. How about a hug for your father?"

But Gary still couldn't move.

Eunice held out a hand. "It's okay, punkin," she said softly.

His father scooped him up into his arms and hugged him hard. Gary felt his father's strength, felt the sandpaper roughness of his beard stubble, and smelled the aftershave lotion that still lingered from that morning's shave. He hugged back with all his might.

At last, they were a family. When Gary went to bed that night—in his own bedroom, underneath a protective tent of mosquito netting—he prayed that being together would mean they would all be happy. But two days later, he started to suspect that would not be the case.

"Servants?" His mother shook her head. "What am I going to do with servants?"

Oscar tugged his uniform belt in place, then gestured to the two Filipinos on the front porch. "Everybody here has servants. They'll do the household duties. Just tell them what you want done. They'll help with the boy, too."

Before he left the house, Oscar fixed Gary with a stern

look. "Don't forget the rules. You stay on the compound unless someone is with you. You be in the house with clean hands by five o'clock. A cannon gets fired at five o'clock every night, so you just be sure you're in here before it goes off. If you're not, you'll be restricted. Understand?"

Gary nodded, too intimidated by his father's military tone to say a word.

Then Oscar left. Eunice looked at the Filipino man and woman still standing on the front porch. Their names were Rom and Maria.

"What am I going to do with servants?" Eunice said again, this time to herself.

It didn't take her long to figure it out, however. Within a week, Rom and Maria were handling the household duties, giving Eunice plenty of time to get to know the other officers' wives. That's when things started to go downhill.

The officers' wives had little to do on the compound, so they often played cards together. As they played, they gossiped about other women and drank tea. But sometimes they drank more than tea, hard drinks like whiskey, gin, and beer. As Eunice got to know the women better, she stayed home less and less. When she did come home, she usually smelled of alcohol.

Oscar drank, too, though not while he was working. When he came home, he and Eunice kept a bottle open most of the night. As his parents became drunk, they would start to argue. Gary learned to stay quiet and tried not to hear the fights that often raged in the next room. The happy family life he had hoped for was quickly dissolving.

The days and weeks ticked by. Then, suddenly, it was a week before Christmas.

Eunice seemed to pull herself together during the holiday season. She planned to make a small tree out of banana leaves and showed Gary how to make decorations out of tin foil and cut-up coffee cans.

But it was all for nothing. A typhoon was approaching! When news of the storm reached the island, Gary's father hurried home to tell his family to get ready. Then he left to tend to some final details at work. Rom left immediately to be with his wife and children. Maria, Eunice, and Gary gathered blankets, food, and water. Ryland picked them up and drove them to the shelter, a big building that had been a rich man's house before the war.

Gary kept looking at the sky, trying to catch a glimpse of the typhoon. But he couldn't see any sign of it. It wasn't until they were safely in the basement, packed in with crowds of others, that the storm hit.

The winds were ferocious, ripping trees apart and tearing huge sheets of tin from the roofs of houses. At dawn, Gary stood at a casement window, watching the destruction as it happened. That's when he saw the man running across the street—and the piece of tin flying through the air toward him.

His mouth dry with horror, he saw the tin slice the man in half like an enormous knife, killing him instantly. He realized then, and would never forget, how powerful and merciless the weather could be. He left the window to cry in his mother's arms.

When the storm was finally over, the village compound and all the houses had to be rebuilt. But soon, too soon, life picked up where it had left off.

Rom was taking care of Gary nearly single-handedly now. Gary had explored the compound as far as he dared on his own. Now he insisted Rom take him to farther places, places made dangerous by the war. Rom, a servant, didn't dare disobey. And Gary, left to his own devices for so long, ignored Rom's warnings.

On a bike Rom had scavenged, they traveled outside the compound. From the moment he first moved off soil controlled by the United States Army, Gary turned native.

It didn't happen all at once. The first steps were small, like when he paid a Filipino boy for a ride on the boy's water buffalo and sampled the food in the marketplace. Then he and Rom started visiting Rom's wife and family. They lived in a two-room shack and ate rice and mashed sardines with their hands. Out in the streets, he learned about the black market and soon was stealing food and cigarettes from his house to sell. He learned to speak the language, to stand like a Filipino on one leg with the foot of the other tucked behind his knee, to squat in the dust and watch the American soldiers with distrust.

He listened to Rom tell stories about the war. One terrible story in particular stuck in his imagination.

"There is a cave where Japanese soldiers were buried alive by American soldiers," he told Gary one day. "It is a very bad place."

Gary didn't care. He had already seen a lot of bad things in his life; now he wanted to see the cave. So, when he caught Rom stealing, Gary blackmailed Rom into taking him.

Gary and Rom had to wade through waist-high grass to reach the cave, which was set back in the jungle near a small white church. When they came to the hill that held the cave, Gary broke free from Rom, ignoring his shout to stop, and wormed his way into the cave's tiny entrance.

He had entered a chamber of horrors. At first, his body blocked the sunlight and he couldn't see inside. But then he stood up and light illuminated the cave's interior. The smell of decay hung thick in the air. Bones, skulls, and rags of uniforms littered the floor. To Gary's horror, the floor seemed to move.

A large furry mass darted through the tangle of skeletons. Then another, and another, and another. There were so many rats inside the cave that Gary couldn't take them all in. He stared at them as they darted in and out of the shadows—then the sunlight vanished and Gary screamed.

It was Rom, coming after him. Rom knew what was inside the cave and had tried to keep Gary from it. Now Gary wanted to be as far away from the cave as possible.

He ran and ran, back through the jungle to the place they had left the bike. He threw up, tried to breathe clean air into his lungs, and cried from the fear of what he had seen. When he finally settled down, he and Rom rode silently home to number twenty-six, never speaking of the cave again.

Life continued to unravel at home, though occasionally things were good. Gary and his parents took a vacation to the mountains. On the way, Gary's mother bought him a light-colored dog that a native man was about to kill. Gary named him Snowball.

The two were inseparable. Back home after the vacation, Gary played with Snowball inside the compound. Snowball slept with Gary at night. Gary talked to his canine friend and confided his deepest fears and desires.

"I wish Mother and Father wouldn't drink, and I wish we could be like a regular family," he would whisper in Snowball's ear. The dog would cock his head and seem to listen.

Snowball was Gary's first dog, and though their time together was cut short when Snowball was hit by an army truck, Gary never forgot the bond that he and Snowball shared.

And so the months went by, one after another, until it was Christmas time again. One Christmas had been destroyed by the typhoon. This year, Eunice decided Christmas would be done right.

She managed to find a real evergreen tree and decorated it with Gary's help. She baked traditional Christmas foods, too. She stayed home instead of going out with the officers' wives. But her efforts were too little, too late.

By this time, Gary was so used to riding with Rom in and out of the compound that he couldn't just drop his routine. Rather than stay at home alone, Eunice went back to partying with the officers' wives.

The day before Christmas, Eunice stayed out drinking with her friends. Gary stayed in his room when he heard her come in. She continued to drink until his father came home.

Gary came out when he heard his father. His parents were in the kitchen.

"It's almost Christmas. Let's have a nice dinner," his mother said as brightly as she could. The words were slurred with drink, but she had a smile on her face so Gary tried to pretend he didn't notice.

But dinner was far from nice—ham from a can that was stone cold because Eunice forgot to turn on the oven, and cold potato salad. Both parents were drinking steadily.

It was after dinner that Eunice went crazy. First, she insisted that it was time to decorate the tree. Although the tree had been decorated a week before, Gary did as he had been told, taking ornaments off and putting them back on.

Meanwhile, Eunice looked out the window, then turned to fix Oscar with a cold stare.

"Where's the snow?" she asked accusingly.

Oscar didn't reply, just took another swig from his glass of whiskey.

"Where's the snow?" she said again, angrier this time.

Oscar rolled his eyes. "We're in the tropics," he said. "Remember?"

Eunice threw her drink at him, then walked frantically around the house. She found a large bag of cotton balls in the bathroom and tore it open. Back in the living room, she flung handful after handful of cotton into the air, hissing, "Snow. Snow," as the white tufts gently fell to the floor.

Gary was frightened and sensed that for once, his father was, too. Oscar restrained Eunice and put her to bed. Gary put himself to bed, without a thought about the fact that the next day was Christmas.

When he got up the next morning, cotton still littered the floor. Eunice was drinking coffee in the kitchen. Gary cautiously approached her.

"Merry Christmas," he said.

Eunice's eyes welled up. "Oh, punkin, I've got something to tell you. We're leaving this place. Your daddy's going to stay here for a few weeks longer, but then he's going to join us and we'll be a family again back home."

Gary was confused at first. Home? They were home, weren't they? Then he realized she meant Minnesota, that they were returning to the United States.

Just before the year 1949 began, Gary took one last look at number twenty-six. Then he climbed into the jeep that took his mother and him to the airport, where they boarded a plane for home.

Chapter Five
Being Farmed Out

We live on a farm on the edge of a forest that reaches from our door in Minnesota all the way up to Hudson's Bay. Uncle David says the trees there are stunted and small, the people are short and round, and the polar bears have a taste for human flesh. That's how Uncle David says it when he goes into his stories. He says he's seen such things . . . but that's for later.

The Winter Room

The fighting and drinking that had started in the Philippines continued in Minnesota. Money was tight— and would get tighter as the years went on. Oscar tried but failed to raise chickens. Eunice paid little attention to her son. Gary was left to fend for himself most days, though there were times Oscar and Eunice found it even easier to ship him off to relatives.

In 1950, when he was eleven years old, Gary was sent to his mother's cousin's farm in northern Minnesota to live for the summer. Home life being what it was, Gary figured life on a farm couldn't be much worse.

In fact, it proved to be better—much better, in many ways. For it was with these relatives that Gary first experienced what a real family was like. He learned something about himself, too: that he had enough backbone to handle the difficult sun-up to sun-down routine of farm life. Best of all, he had fun.

His mother's cousin, whom he called "uncle," was married and had two children, a girl and a boy. The boy was a year younger than Gary, but extremely knowledgeable about farm life. Right from the start, he sniffed out Gary's lack of knowledge—and his gullibility—and used them to his advantage.

"This is a separator," his cousin explained to Gary his first day on the farm. He pointed to a machine with a stainless steel bowl filled with milk on one side, and two spigots leading into urns on the other. Between them was a handle. "Milk gets poured in here. You turn the handle and the machine separates the milk from the cream. Easy, right?"

Overcome by shyness and a desire to fit in, Gary simply nodded.

"Okay! Then you take the first shift and I'll take the second." Before Gary could reply, his cousin vanished.

Gary started turning the crank. It moved slowly, as if it was stuck. Finally, though, he got a rhythm going.

He cranked for what seemed like hours. His uncle, aunt, and a farmworker continually replenished the milk supply in the bowl and replaced the full cans of separated milk and cream with empty ones whenever necessary.

Suddenly his cousin reappeared. "My turn," he said. Gary gratefully let go of the handle. As he massaged his sore arms, his aunt dumped another pail of milk into the bowl.

"That's it," she said, wiping her forehead. "Finish that up, and we'll grab a bite to eat."

It was only then that Gary realized his cousin had duped him into separating nearly the whole day's milk. Though he was furious at the time, he soon learned that his cousin's mischievous nature could be fun as well as devious.

His cousin had a matter-of-fact way of explaining totally insane ideas, and making them sound so perfectly reasonable and interesting, that Gary went along with most of his schemes. He talked Gary into helping him play Tarzan by jumping off the barnyard roof holding a threadbare rope. He convinced Gary to ambush and attack the pigs who were contently wallowing in their muck (content, that is, until two screaming boys leaped on them). When he was sure he could land safely on the back of a workhorse after jumping from the granary window, Gary's job was to hold the huge animal steady.

Each adventure ended in delicious, dirt-filled, black-and-blue, cuts-and-scrapes disaster. And Gary loved every minute of it.

Along with these disasters with his cousin came hard work on the farm and fun outings with the family. Gary grew to love the life and the people, and felt like he belonged for the first time.

Then summer suddenly ended and Gary had to return to his parents. It was the last thing on earth he wanted to do. The family gathered around the car that would take

Gary away—all except for his cousin, who was nowhere to be found.

Gary climbed into the car after saying his good-byes. That's when his cousin appeared.

"Ya stupid gooner," he said, his voice sounding strange. Gary looked closely at him, and saw that his fearless cousin was crying. Gary started crying too, partly from knowing that his cousin was going to miss him as much as he was going to miss him.

There was nothing either of them could do. Gary had to return to his parents, for the school year was due to begin soon. So Gary left, knowing that school meant ridicule for a haircut that wouldn't look right, for clothes that wouldn't fit right, for poor grades, for being from the wrong part of town. But deep down inside, he carried with him the knowledge that he had one friend in the world who didn't care about all that.

Gary was to spend many months at other relatives' farms throughout his teenage years. Farm life was far from easy. Each season brought a new set of chores: preparing the fields and sowing the crops in the spring and early summer; slaughtering hogs and harvesting the crops in the fall; and tending the cows, pigs, chickens, sheep, and horses all year long. Though Gary was one more mouth to feed, he was also another set of hands to help with the constant work, so most of the relatives welcomed him.

And it wasn't all hard work. At one farm, he listened to an uncle retell stories of the old country, Norway, and of the early years of living in Minnesota—tales that made the nights come alive with romance and heroism, though the uncle insisted they were all true. At the end of a long day, those stories made the evenings a time of relaxation and comfort.

Gary tucked away the memories of those nights and days on the farm, never dreaming at the time that one day he would take them out, dust them off, and unfold them for others to enjoy.

Chapter Six
A Dog in the Darkness

I am — I say this with some pride and a little wonder — a "dog person." I make no excuses for unabashedly loving them. . . .

dedication to My Life in Dog Years

When Gary arrived home, nothing had changed. His parents were still drinking and money was still tight. At school Gary found the classes uninteresting. He didn't make friends easily so he spent much of his time alone, building model airplanes or reading comics when he couldn't go outside.

He was outdoors as much as he could be, though, because the trees and rivers didn't judge him and didn't face each day with a drink in hand. When he was twelve, an uncle gave him a Remington .22 rifle. Gary learned to hunt and soon disappeared into the woods every chance he could. One day, while hunting, he made a friend.

The friend was not a person, but a dog. Gary had never forgotten Snowball, and though this dog was as different from Snowball as the Philippines were from Minnesota, a strong bond grew between them.

It was fall when Gary met the black Labrador. He had arisen at three in the morning to go duck hunting. After packing a breakfast, he grabbed his gun and headed out into the darkness.

It was raining. Gary was climbing up the riverbank, concentrating on not slipping back down, when a large shadow moved near him and said, "Woof."

Gary was so startled he nearly dropped his breakfast and his gun. He thought for sure he had just come face to face with a bear. He stumbled back down the embankment, fumbled for his gun, and aimed.

Just then, the light changed enough for him to see the shadow more clearly. It wasn't a bear. It was a dog. Gary lowered his gun—remembering only then that it wasn't even loaded yet anyway—and scrambled back up the bank to the dog.

"Whose dog are you?" Gary asked the Lab. The dog sat down. Gary suspected the dog belonged to another hunter who was somewhere about, so he called out. But no one answered and the dog still sat.

As the light grew stronger, Gary could see that the dog was not a stray. It was too well fed and too well behaved.

On impulse, Gary asked, "Would you like to go hunting with me?"

His question was answered with a few quick thumps of the dog's tail.

"All right then, let's see what you're made of." Gary checked his gun, cleared some mud out of the bore, then started off again.

The dog came along but stayed far from Gary, even when Gary settled down to wait for a shot. Just as Gary was going to call him closer, the dog flushed two mallards out of the tall grass. Gary had loaded his gun, and now had a perfect shot at the ducks.

Crack! The gun exploded and the bullet hit one of the ducks. It spiraled down, landing with a splash in the river.

"Drat!" Gary muttered. He knew from past experience that he would either have to wade in the frigid water to get the duck—not something he was likely to do—or hope that the current would eventually float the bird to him.

He did neither. Moments after the duck hit the water, the dog sprang into action. He plunged into the river, swam with strong strokes to the bird, took it gently in his mouth, and returned to Gary.

Gary had never hunted with a dog before. He watched the whole thing with fascination.

When the dog dropped the duck at Gary's feet, Gary saw that he was wearing a collar with a tag. Slowly, so as not to frighten the dog, Gary reached for the tag. He turned it over with his fingers and read, *My name is Ike.* No address, no owner's name, no telephone number.

"Well, Ike," Gary said. "Whoever trained you sure knew what he or she was doing." He picked up the bird. "And thanks for getting my duck for me."

From that morning through the rest of the fall, Gary and Ike hunted together. Gary never knew where Ike went when the hunt was done, but he did know that Ike was the best friend he had. He would talk to the Lab as he had talked to Snowball, and when he camped out, Ike would stay with him through the night.

Then one morning Ike didn't show up. Gary tried to pretend it didn't matter. But it did, and it took him a long time to get over the fact that Ike wasn't coming back. Thirty years later, he found out what had happened to Ike; that fall, however, all he knew was that he had lost his best friend.

Chapter Seven
Growing Up Outdoors

He had to "invent" the bow and arrow—he almost laughed as he moved out of the water and put his shoes on. . . . Maybe that was how it really happened, way back when—some primitive man tried to spear fish and it didn't work and he "invented" the bow and arrow. Maybe it was always that way, discoveries happened because they needed to happen.

Hatchet

Although Gary had a tough time making friends at school, he wasn't the only boy in town to come from a poor home. Soon, he teamed up with some of the others; and while he didn't become close friends with many of them, these relationships and his own inner strength helped him survive.

With these boys, Gary took to the woods and the streams. He became an accomplished hunter. One winter, he impressed his buddies by tracking a deer, stealing up to it slowly, silently, and touching it.

But the moment the ice melted and winter turned to spring, fishing became their obsession. Fishing was fun. It took talent, and if you had that talent, you could make money because people who didn't fish wanted to eat fish.

Catching the fish the people wanted to eat wasn't easy, however—especially since Gary and his buddies were using heavy, outdated rods, rusty reels, some homemade lures, and a can of worms. Sometimes, their equipment was as simple as a barbed spear or a bow and arrow.

"C'mon, we got to get a move on or the other guys will get all the sucker fish," Gary's friends called to him.

Gary pounded out of the apartment carrying his bow and arrow. Around his neck was a gunnysack for holding the suckers he was going to catch. He had spare sacks already loaded onto his bike. As the door slammed behind him, he didn't bother to call out to his parents to let them know where he was going.

"Those ditches looked loaded with suckers yesterday," Gary commented as he and the other boys mounted their bikes. His friends knew he was talking about the thirty-mile-long drainage ditches that had been carved out years earlier around and through the flat farmlands. Suckers, thick-lipped freshwater fish, had somehow found their way into the man-made waterholes; in time, the shallow ditches became their spawning areas.

"Well, let's go get 'em!" one of the boys yelled. He stood on his bike and pedaled with all his might. The other boys followed, giving a war whoop from time to time. When they reached the ditches, though, they quieted down. Fishing was serious business, after all.

Gary laid his bike on the ground with the others. He took his bow and examined it. The string was good and taut, so he put it aside and picked up the arrow. The cedar shaft he had bought for a nickel was still strong, though the turkey feathers were looking a little worn. He'd have to replace those soon. The arrow point was sharp, and the tiny nail he had driven through it to make a barb was secure. He was ready.

He lowered down into the ditch, bracing himself for the icy water. The minute he slid in, his toes and ankles turned numb and his skin puckered into gooseflesh. To help him endure the cold, he thought about the fire they would build later.

Once in the ditch, he trailed his nocked arrow in the water and searched for suckers. Nearby, one of his buddies was doing the same thing, only he was using a barbed spear. Both boys knew the closer they got to the fish with the points of their weapons, the more likely they were to get one. They tried not to let the water play tricks on their eyes, making a fish seem to be directly under the point when really it was off to one side.

Suddenly, Gary spotted a sucker in good range. He let his arrow fly. It struck true, piercing the fish and continuing through until it pinned the fish to the ground below. Gary reached in, found the arrow, and pulled up his catch. He carefully removed it from the arrow and put it in his gunnysack. Then he nocked the arrow again and got ready for the next one.

All day long, Gary fished with his friends, sitting by the fire when the cold water became too much to bear, and gutting fish to make more room in the gunnysack. By the time the light started to dim, his gunnysacks were bursting. He loaded them onto his bike and started pushing it. But he wasn't going home. He and the other boys were headed for the smoke shed.

The smoke shed was owned by an old man who charged the boys half their catch to smoke their fish. It was a high price to pay, but since the boys could do what they wanted with the other half, they agreed to the arrangement.

The smoking process lasted a few days. Gary and the other boys took shifts manning the shed. When the fish was smoked, Gary took what was left of his catch and started for home.

"You gonna sell yours?" one of the boys asked him.

"Sure, aren't you? Gonna get rich, too," Gary replied. But even as he said it, he knew it wouldn't happen—not because people wouldn't pay good money for the delicately smoked fish, but because he wanted to eat the fish himself. He could almost taste the smoky, salty, fishy flavor. His mouth watered as he shoved off.

Oh well, he said to himself. There are always more. If not suckers, then northern pike, or sunfish, or bullheads. Always more. The streams and woods will always be here for me. And they always were, then and in his future.

Chapter Eight
A Writer Is Born

*"And I thought, 'I can't believe I've done this to myself where
I'm going to sit in back of this console for the rest of my life!'"*
Gary Paulsen
interview with Kay Miller
Minneapolis Star-Tribune Sunday Magazine (1988)

Gary continued to depend on the woods and rivers for
solace during his teenage years. But one year, being at
home was too much to bear.

When he was sixteen, he ran away from home, hitch-hiked to the farmlands of North Dakota, and took a job hoeing sugar beets. The work was dreadful—standing in the hot fields all day, mindlessly lopping the tops off of beets through row after row and acre after acre of dusty farmland—and Gary collapsed on the floor of a rough shed with other workers each night, sapped of his strength, both mental and physical. Something deep inside told him to leave, that he could do just that, but somehow when the next morning came he was up and working the beets again.

Then he learned that he was being charged money for sleeping on the floor of the shed and for the meager food he was fed each day—money that was being automatically deducted from his earnings! When Gary found out, he snapped, fought violently with the overseer, and ran off. While on the road, he was picked up by some carnival folk who took him under their wing. For the rest of the summer, Gary was a "carnie."

He learned the tricks of the trade, like letting players win at the games the first few times so they would keep spending their money to play, thinking the next game they'd surely win again. He learned how to "shill"—to pretend he was a customer and talk up one of the side-shows to get everyone around him interested enough to pay—and how to run the tiltawhirl. He made money and friends, but he realized that the carnival life wasn't for him after all. So, sadly and reluctantly, with nowhere else to turn, he went home.

He struggled through the rest of high school, barely graduating with a D minus average in 1957. He had been accepted into Bemidji State Teacher's College, but after one semester (to the surprise of no one who knew him in school), he flunked out. At nineteen years old, with no where to go, he joined the army.

He had basic training in Fort Carson, Colorado, then spent time in Oklahoma and various army bases in Texas, the last one being Fort Bliss. Three years and some months after he signed up, Gary was honorably discharged, a tougher, more determined man. He had hated the Army, but at least it had given him some skills with which he could earn a living.

He was knowledgeable enough in electrical engineering to land a job at an aerospace company. He worked for different companies in the next few years; it was while working for a deep-space tracking station in California that his life took a sudden and completely unexpected turn.

Gary sat at his station. In front of him were the console and computers he used to monitor the sky. It was nighttime, and he was bored. He picked up a magazine and started to read.

The article he read was about test-flying a new airplane. The article was well-written and informative, but the airplane wasn't what interested him. As he read, his mind began to twitch as a new, bold thought fluttered through it. When he finished the article, he let the magazine drop on the console.

What a way to make a living, he thought. *Writing about something you like and getting paid for it!*

At that moment, Gary Paulsen made a decision. He was not meant to be an electrical engineer, to fiddle with knobs and buttons all day. He was supposed to be a writer.

Without further hesitation or deeper thought, Gary left his post. He drove to the guard shack and handed in his security badge. Then he drove the company car to a nearby gas station, left it there for the company to pick up, and walked home.

There was only one problem—Gary didn't know the first thing about writing. Here he was, a man who had barely finished high school, had flunked out of college, and had spent the last few years of his life as a soldier and electrical engineer. Those were hardly the qualifications one would expect to find on a writer's resume.

But Gary didn't let that stop him. He took a fresh sheet of paper and typed his first real piece of fiction: a resume that more or less stated that he had a wide range of editorial experience.

While living in Hollywood, he mailed his resume to many places. Finally, he landed a job with a magazine publisher. His education as a writer had begun.

Gary worked hard at the magazine every day, soaking up knowledge as quickly as he could. He divided his time between writing articles for the ten different magazines the company published and editing pieces written by others.

He worked hard at night, too, crafting his own short stories. But unlike the writing he did for the magazine, he had no idea if his own work could be published or if it was even any good at all. One day, he decided he had to find out. He gathered together a few of his stories and brought them to the magazine.

Feeling a little nervous, he knocked on the door of a coworker's office.

"Say, Dick," Gary said, "would you look over this thing I wrote? It's not for the magazine, but if you could just give me your impression of it, I'd appreciate it." He dropped the sheaf of papers on Dick Ashby's desk.

Dick was one of the people who edited Gary's work at the magazine. He also wrote his own pieces. Gary had chosen him because he thought Dick was one of the best writers he had ever read, and because Dick seemed like he'd be sympathetic. Dick agreed to take a look.

From then on, Gary had Dick look at much of what he wrote. He wanted to get more than one person's opinion, so he asked two other coworkers, Ray Locke and Jared Rutter, to review his stories, too. Their criticisms, suggestions, and encouragement guided Gary's fledgling writing career.

With such a support system, Gary started working even harder to become a writer. Soon, his job at the magazine and his Hollywood lifestyle became distractions that cut into his writing time. He decided to return to Minnesota so he could concentrate solely on his writing.

He had little money saved so the best housing he could afford in Minnesota was a small cabin on a lake. It cost him twenty-five dollars a month to live there. He ate rabbits that he snared and fish that he speared in the lake. Every so often someone would give him food, like a huge sack of potatoes or a deer. He barely got by, but without the temptations of Hollywood and the rigors of a regular job, Gary found he could write better.

He wrote all winter long, finally completing the manuscript for an adult nonfiction book, a series of humorous essays about the missile industry called *Some Birds Don't Fly*. He sold it in the spring of 1967. Seven months later, he had written and sold a second book, his first middle grade novel, called *Mr. Tucket*. At long last, Gary could honestly call himself a published author!

With money from the books in hand, Gary made another life-changing decision. He bought a boat and moved back to California.

The boat-home lasted all of six months before Gary decided it was time to move yet again. He wanted to surround himself with other like-minded authors and artists. He had heard that Taos, New Mexico, was the place to go.

In 1968, Taos was a mecca for artists. People there experimented with many different ways of interpreting the world around them—through words, through paintings, through sculpture, and through other art forms. Gary was sure it was just the place for him to stretch his mind to the fullest.

But it was in Taos that Gary Paulsen nearly lost all that he had worked so hard to achieve.

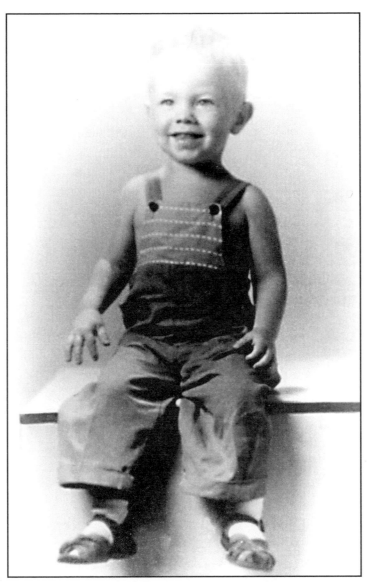

Gary, age 2, in Minnesota in 1941

Gary at age 3

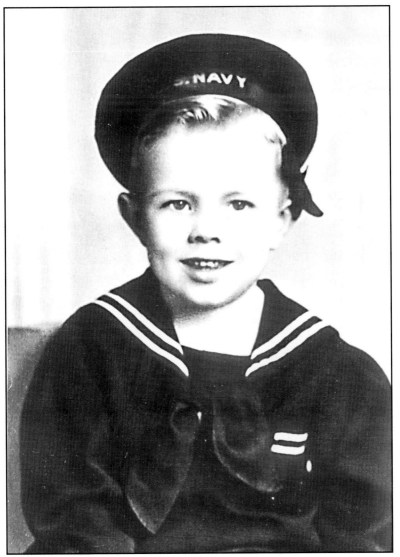

Gary at age 4

Gary in 1945 in front of the house in Manila

Gary in 1947 in the Phillipines

Gary's high school yearbook photo, 1957

*Gary (on the right) with author Theodore Taylor
and sled dogs in Minnesota in the 1980s*

*Gary tending to one of
his sled dogs*

Gary in 1992 with Josh, the border collie

Gary alongside the car he partially built, the Blakely Bearcat, the inspiration for his book, The Car

Gary, during a rare moment of rest, on board his sailboat

Gary and a friend in Alaska in 1995

Gary on board his catamaran

Gary's wife, Ruth Wright Paulsen

Chapter Nine
Crawling In and Out of the Bottle

"In Taos, I really went for it, and within a year or year-and-a-half, I became an alcoholic drinker."

Gary Paulsen
interview with Gary M. Salver for
Presenting Gary Paulsen

Gary rolled over in bed and started to cough violently. He swung his feet out of bed and stumbled to the bathroom, still hacking. His mouth filled with saliva as he reached the toilet just in time to throw up.

He raised his head, swiping at his mouth with the back of his hand. Avoiding the medicine cabinet mirror, he filled a glass with water, took a swig, and swished it around in his mouth. Then he spat the water back into the sink.

Gary had been living in Taos for several months. During that time, he had written . . . nothing. Nothing worth publishing. Nothing worth showing anyone. Nothing to remind himself and others that he was a published author.

Instead, Gary had followed in his parents' footsteps and started drinking—hard, as they had, and daily. It had cost him his creative drive.

Drinking hadn't been the only obstacle in Gary's career path, though it was by far the biggest. He had also been the subject of an investigation by the Federal Bureau of Investigation—the FBI. Unbeknownst to Gary, his first published book, *Some Birds Don't Fly*, contained information the government hadn't wished to be made public. The FBI had been curious to know how Gary had come by such classified information. They had made life rather unpleasant for him until they were convinced he had come by his knowledge honestly, and written about it innocently.

Gary coughed once more, then put the glass down and returned to the bedroom. *At least the Feds aren't on my back anymore,* he said to himself in an attempt to buoy his spirits. He pulled on his clothes for the day—clothes just right for his job as a construction worker. Then he climbed into his car, which smelled of the whiskey he had consumed the night before, and drove to work.

The days and weeks and months continued to pass in this way. The bottles seemed to empty themselves as Gary moved from being a drinker to being a drunk. When he did write, it was little more than a short story or a magazine article. He just didn't have the stamina to pull off a book-length work.

One day, just after he cashed a check for twenty dollars for a short story he'd written, he was standing in line at the post office. The door opened and in walked two familiar faces—FBI agents.

Oh, no, they're coming for me again, Gary thought, suddenly panicked. *What should I do?*

He fingered his wallet with the twenty dollars in it. On impulse, he turned to the woman behind him.

"Listen," he said quietly. "Those two guys are Federal agents. I think they're here for me. Could you take my money and hold it for me, just in case?"

The woman was wearing dark glasses, so Gary couldn't see her expression clearly. But she held out her hand and accepted the wallet.

Gary tried to make himself invisible. He needn't have bothered. The agents soon left without giving him a second look.

With a huge sigh of relief, Gary turned to the woman behind him again.

"Thanks," he said, holding out his hand for the wallet.

The woman placed it in his hand, removing her glasses at the same time. When Gary looked into her eyes, something unexpected happened. He fell in love.

Gary finished his business at the post office, then waited until the woman had finished hers, too. He caught up to her as she headed to the door.

"I guess you think I'm a little nuts, huh?" he said sheepishly.

The woman smiled. "We live in an artist's colony," she replied. "I think we all must be a little nuts to be here."

"I'm Gary, Gary Paulsen." He held out his hand.

"Ruth Wright," the woman with the beautiful eyes replied. "I'm an artist."

Gary wanted to say he was a writer, but didn't. Given the fact that he'd written hardly anything lately, how could he say such a thing in all honesty to this woman? Instead, he asked her if she'd go out with him sometime. She agreed.

Ruth and Gary were soon together all the time. A year later, in 1969, they moved to Ruth's home state of Colorado. Two years after that, they were married.

Though Ruth was the light of his life, she couldn't pull him free from his self-destructive drinking. Even when she gave birth to their only child, a son they named Jim, Gary kept drinking. Then one night in 1973, he finally saw how his behavior was damaging his loved ones.

The Paulsens were back in Taos for a visit. Gary had taken Jim with him to a friend's house for a party. The alcohol was flowing freely, as usual, and Gary filled his glass again and again. Soon, he was so drunk that he passed out on a couch. Two-year-old Jim was beside him.

When Gary woke up, he was groggy.

"Where am I?" he croaked to no one in particular. Then he spotted his son sleeping beside him. Suddenly, he was wide awake.

What am I doing? he thought. Shame washed over him. *I'm sleeping on a couch in somebody's house, 370 miles from my home, drinking and laughing and thinking I'm happy. But I'm not.*

He gently picked up Jim, loaded him into the car and, with Ruth, drove back home to Denver that night. On the ride there, he vowed over and over that he was going to quit drinking.

He didn't—at least not that night. Or the next night, or the night after that. He wanted to, desperately wanted to, but didn't have the strength to do it himself. Finally, he called for help.

On May 5, 1973, his and Ruth's third wedding anniversary, Gary stopped drinking for good. It had been six years since he had last written anything of significance. It would be two years more before he would publish another book.

Chapter Ten
Dogs

"Men and dogs are not alike, although some men try to make them so. White men." Oogruk had laughed. "Because they try to make people out of dogs and in this way they make the dogs dumb. But to say that a dog is not smart because it is not as smart as a man is to say that snow is not smart. Dogs are not men. And as dogs, if they are allowed to be dogs, they are often smarter than men."

Dogsong

Once Gary found his way back to his craft, he was unstoppable. He wrote and wrote: adult mysteries, how-to manuals, biographies, sports books, nature books. And he wrote young adult fiction: adventure stories, survival stories, westerns, mysteries. He started to make good money—until a bad deal with a publisher left him and Ruth nearly penniless. Facing poverty, Gary packed up his family and fled to his familiar stomping grounds in Minnesota.

It was cold and snowy in Minnesota. Gary, Ruth, and Jim were living in a shack without plumbing, without electricity, with only a barrel stove for heat. His car had been repossessed, so Gary had no way of getting from place to place except on foot.

To make matters worse, he was sued for libel by a man who claimed he had used him as a character in a novel. The company that published the book didn't like the lawsuit. It stood silent as Gary fought a costly battle by himself. Though he won the suit, the experience was pivotal.

"That's it," Gary said to Ruth in 1975. "I'm through with writing. Here, take my pens and my paper."

Three weeks later, Gary asked for his writing materials back. Even though he wasn't producing anything worth publishing, the pull to write was just too strong. In the meantime, however, Gary needed to do something to bring in money so his family could survive. What he did eventually led to his first great writing success.

Gary had learned how to trap animals when he was growing up. Minnesota paid trappers to run trap lines to help control the destructive beaver and coyote populations. The longer the line, the more money you could make. In 1979, Gary turned back to his childhood skill to help pay the bills.

The work was far from easy. Gary's line was twenty miles long and he covered it all on foot.

"I don't know if I'm going to be able to keep doing this," he told Ruth one evening after returning home, cold and exhausted after a day of running the line.

Fate intervened. A few days later, Gary's friend and neighbor, Bob McWilliams, stopped by.

"How's the line going?" Bob asked.

Gary shook his head. "It's tough work, doing it all on foot," he replied. "Fact is, I'm wondering if it's too tough."

Bob looked thoughtful. Then he said, "Would you be interested in trying to do it on dogsled, instead? I've got an old beat-up sled you could fix up, plus four dogs I can't keep any more. They're nothing special, but they're yours free if you want 'em."

Gary did. He loved dogs and the idea of having company on the line was appealing. And he was good with his hands, so repairing the sled wouldn't be a problem. He accepted Bob's offer.

His life would never be the same. Gary fixed the sled, learned the basics of dog sledding, and expanded his trap line from twenty miles to sixty. But it wasn't the extra money the forty additional miles brought in that changed him. It was the dogs: Storm, Obeah, Yogi, and Columbia.

Wolf-like, driven by an ancient urge to run and pull, too wild ever to live indoors, those dogs opened a door to nature that Gary had never seen or dreamed existed when he'd been growing up.

At first, he drove the dogs as if he could control them and the land they ran through. Then one night, he realized that was exactly the wrong attitude to take. Nature was not meant to be controlled. It was meant to be reveled in, to be marveled at, to be worshipped quietly.

Gary and the dogs were cutting across a three-mile-wide lake. They had been checking the trapline earlier in the evening and were making their way home in the darkness. The air was frigid, so cold it seemed to snap. The stillness was broken only by the soft sounds of the dogs' paws in the snow, the shush of the sled runners, and the jingle of the harness.

The dogs knew where they were going, and Gary allowed himself a moment to look around. The moon was full and splashed a mellow light on the trees, the lake, the dogs, and the steam from the running dogs' mouths. The beauty of the scene took Gary's breath away.

The dogs puffed up a hill to a fork in the trail. A left turn would lead them home. They were still a fair distance away, almost twenty miles, but they could cover the ground in about two or three hours if they kept running at a steady pace.

Gary turned them right. The beauty of the moment was too much for him to leave. He wanted to wallow in it, to make the moment last and last.

It lasted for eight days. Eight days of living off the land, of living with the dogs in the dead of winter. Eight days of not seeing or caring to see another human being.

When Gary did finally return home, Ruth was nearly frantic.

"I thought you'd fallen through the ice!" she cried. "I thought you had drowned!"

But when she saw how moved Gary had been by his experience, she forgave him. She understood who Gary was and she appreciated what he had seen and felt. As an artist, she knew how important it was to stay in tune with beauty when you found it.

Gary added more dogs to his growing kennel and started spending more time running them. By now, he was working nearly eighteen hours a day, fourteen with the dogs, and four with his pen and paper. He brought his notebook and pen to the kennel so he could be near the dogs when he wrote. As he grew to know them, he discovered that every dog had a unique personality. Some were workers, living to pull. Some were bullies. Some were leaders and some were lazy. Most were intelligent. One dog made Gary see the intelligence more clearly than he ever had before.

On that day, Gary sat, notebook in hand, near two dogs, Olaf and Columbia. Both were on chains that allowed them to cover a large circle of territory. Olaf, something of a brute, had a history of trying to pick fights with Columbia. Today, Columbia would get his revenge.

Columbia had a bone with a small scrap of meat still on it. Olaf wanted that bone. As Gary watched, Columbia nosed the bone closer and closer to Olaf. Olaf licked his chops, anticipating the juicy morsel. He pulled at his chain until he had pulled as far as he could go.

That's when Columbia stopped and sat down. Olaf stretched his paw out and got one claw on the bone. But that was it. Columbia had managed to judge the exact spot to leave the bone so it would be *just* out of Olaf's reach.

Gary swore Columbia was laughing at Olaf. Seeing that intelligence made him realize something very important. He tried to sum up his revelation for Ruth.

"If a dog can make up such a complicated joke—I mean, Columbia had to think about what would make a bully like Olaf crazy, then work out where to leave the bone, and let's not forget he had to *not eat the bone himself*—then that says something about how animals' minds work, don't you think? And it can't be just dogs that can think like that. Other animals, like wolves, deer, beaver, coyote, you name it. They all have brains and maybe their brains can't think up jokes like that but they do think."

Ruth nodded slowly, seeing what he was seeing.

"I guess what I'm saying is, I'd better start making

enough money by writing for us to live on. Because I can't trap any more. I can't kill any more."

And still Ruth nodded, because she understood.

Gary stopped running the trap line, but he didn't stop running the dogs. They continued to follow their trails together, though Gary felt somewhat silly since they didn't have a reason for being there.

The dogs didn't seem to mind. Gary cared for them, let them follow their instinctive nature to run, and they were loyal to him. Any kindness he showed them was repaid a hundred times over. This was especially true the day Gary made a mistake that nearly cost him his life.

Gary and the dogs were running up a steep trail Gary had never been on before. The dogs were excited and moving at full steam. Then the trail ended.

Or rather, it shot downward about fifty feet, into a small canyon cut by a stream. Any other time, Gary would have admired the beauty of the spot, especially the small waterfall at one end. But now the canyon became a torture chamber.

The sled, the dogs, and Gary were moving so fast that the earth seemed to drop out from under them. The dogs found the ground again, but Gary launched off the sled as if from a cannon.

Something sharp tore at his knee as he flew through the air. He landed hard and tumbled down the twenty-foot waterfall. A moment later, he hit the ground again. His torn knee was directly beneath him. Pain exploded and consumed his brain, driving away all sane thought for minutes.

When reason returned, Gary almost wished it hadn't. He couldn't walk, it was the dead of winter, and he was miles from home. The dogs, he knew, would have continued to run for home. He couldn't blame them; it was their nature to do so. But it left him completely alone and completely helpless.

He shut his eyes, cursing himself for not having been more careful, then cursing himself again for wasting energy on such fruitless thoughts. That's when he heard the small whine.

His eyes flew open, unable to believe what they saw. His lead dog, Obeah, was at the top of the waterfall. Behind him was the rest of the team. The dogs hadn't run. But how could they possibly help? He was down here, and they were up there.

Obeah took matters into hand. He dragged the team away from the waterfall, through a stand of cockleburs, to jockey them into better position closer to Gary. Then slowly, he guided them along until they reached Gary.

Gary hugged Obeah hard, nestling his windblown and scratched face into his fur. Duberry, another dog, gently licked at Gary's wound as if to clean it. When she was done, Gary knew he had to move.

In agony still, he untangled the dogs and unloaded the sled until he had enough room to crawl onto it. He strapped himself in, then weakly gave the dogs the command to go home. They took him there, moving surefootedly across the frozen land.

Gary never forgot the wonderful sight of Obeah's face peering down at him from above the waterfall. His love for the dogs and for dog sledding was greater than ever. He couldn't deny that dog sledding through the forests of Minnesota without a reason didn't make much sense. But then he read something that gave him a reason.

It was an article about a dog sled race in Alaska called the Iditarod. The Iditarod wasn't just any old race. It was a brutal trek across more than one thousand miles of barren, frigid, Alaskan tundra, with nothing more than your dog team and your sled to get you from Anchorage to Nome.

The moment Gary read the article, he knew he had to run that race.

Chapter Eleven
Training for the Race of a Lifetime

He was one of the first dogs and taught me the most and as we worked together he came to know me better than perhaps even my own family. He could look once over his shoulders and tell how I was feeling, tell how far we were to run, how fast we had to run—knew it all.

Woodsong

Once he had made the decision to run the Iditarod, Gary threw himself and his dogs into training. He took the dogs and sled out and ran them for hours on end. When the snow was gone, he mounted a sled on wheels and ran still more, determined to be prepared to run the race in 1983.

Teaching the dogs was only a part of what it would take to make it to Alaska. Money was the other part. Gary was making a modest living as a writer, but he didn't have enough extra money to get to Alaska or to pay for the supplies he would need. Then the people in the nearby town of Bemidji heard what he was trying to do. They rallied around him, holding raffles and dances to raise money. With their help, Gary eventually had enough to enter the Iditarod.

But the fund raisers would all have been for nothing if his dogs weren't ready. Gary began a rigorous training program to get the dogs—and himself—ready for the race.

The bond between Gary and his dogs grew stronger with every mile they covered. Two dogs in particular stood out: Cookie for the heart she showed each time she was put in harness, and Storm for the knowledge and humor he passed on to Gary.

Cookie was given to Gary by a man who thought she was too sick to be of any use.

"She'll probably die on you," the man told Gary when he dropped Cookie off. "But if anyone can make a go of her, you can."

Gary looked down at the animal at his feet. She was truly pathetic-looking: thin to the point of emaciation, scraggly-haired, and weak. But Gary thought he knew what the problem was. She had worms.

Gary had learned that sled dogs are born with worms. If left untreated, the condition can be fatal. Gary realized that's what was happening to Cookie.

He started her on worm treatments right away. In addition, he fed her protein-rich, fatty beaver meat—as much as she wanted. Soon, Cookie responded. Her fur grew in and she gained strength. Gary decided it was time to try her out in the team.

He harnessed Cookie toward the back of the line, near the sled, where he could watch her closely. He was astounded to see the energy she put into the run. Cookie hadn't been trained to run long distances, only short sprints. But she took to the new routine as if she had been born to it. Before long, Gary moved Cookie to the position of lead dog.

"I can't believe the change in her," Ruth marveled one day as she stood near Cookie's spot in the kennel, watching the dog romp and jump. Gary agreed and said a silent word of thanks to the man who had given up on Cookie.

He had good reason to thank that man again one wintry day. That was the day Cookie saved his life.

Gary was giving the dogs a chance to sleep after a long run. They were on a lake frozen solid by the frigid Minnesota air. At least Gary thought the ice was solid.

He was standing over a beaver dam. The ice near the dam had been worn thin by the beavers' backs as they swam back and forth underneath it in their quest for food. Gary wasn't paying attention and he missed the telltale signs that he was on thin ice.

Gary screamed as the ice collapsed beneath him. He instinctively grabbed hold of a rope attached to the sled. But the rope was of little help. Gary sank like a stone into the icy water.

As he went down, he locked eyes with Cookie.

Later, Gary would wonder what Cookie had seen in his eyes that moment. Right now, though, the only thought in Gary's head was, "I am going to die."

Then the rope in his hands tightened and started to

move. Gary clung to it and slowly felt himself being pulled up and out. Cookie had forced the other dogs, still harnessed to the sled and reluctant to get up from their rest, to their feet. She urged them on until Gary was safely back on solid ice.

As Gary quickly built a fire to warm his soaking-wet body, he kept looking at Cookie. What had passed through her mind when she saw him go through the ice? Had she simply reacted when she heard him holler, or was it something more, a greater understanding that Gary was in trouble and would die unless she acted?

When Gary told of the incident later, he tried to make light of it. "She must have thought, 'The dummy went through the ice, so now I have to pull the dummy out.'" But deep down, he couldn't help thinking that Cookie had seen the terror in his eyes and had acted because she could not ignore his plea for help.

Cookie would always hold a special place in Gary's heart, not just for that rescue but for the meaning she brought to his life. Together they would share many experiences on and off the trail, learning to trust and love one another. When Cookie retired, she became the only dog Gary brought out of the kennel and into his house. When she died, Gary felt a little piece of himself had died, too.

Unlike Cookie, Storm wasn't a lead dog, but he was a strong puller whose back humped with exertion every time a run began. He lived to pull and loved to go the long distances, but sometimes he got bored.

Once, when boredom overtook him, he played a trick

on the dog next to him. While the other dog was concentrating on the run, Storm turned his head and snuffed cold air into the dog's ear.

Startled, the dog whipped his head around and stared at Storm. But Storm was once again the serious sled dog, eyes front and muscles straining. Gary, however, could swear he saw Storm laughing. And Storm must have liked the reaction his joke got because he played it over and over again, on different days, under different circumstances, and on different dogs.

He played tricks on Gary, too. Once, Gary had stopped to make a repair on a harness. The sun was out, and he was warm, so when he stooped down next to the team, he took off his hat. When the repair was done, he turned to pick up the hat—but it was gone.

Gary searched everywhere, but he couldn't find the hat. Scratching his head, and wondering if maybe he hadn't had the hat after all, he prepared to start the team again. Overanxious from their wait, the team lunged forward before Gary was fully on the runners.

"Whoa!" he yelled, grabbing for the snow hook, a device that acts like an anchor when the dogs aren't running. The hook dragged and skipped in the snow and suddenly Gary saw a flash of color.

He stopped the dogs and got off the sled to see what the color was. It was his hat! But how had it gotten buried in the snow?

Gary retraced his steps.

"I squatted here to fix the harness," he mumbled to himself. "I took off my hat and put it down there." He turned slightly and pretended to lay his hat on the ground behind him. Behind him—and beside Storm.

In a flash, he realized that Storm had to have been the culprit. But what a thief! In the little time it had taken Gary to repair the harness, Storm had stolen the hat, quietly buried it just off the trail, *smoothed the snow over the spot so it didn't stand out*, then sat back down to stare innocently out into space as Gary started to look for his hat. Gary brushed the snow off the hat, shaking his head in wonder.

Then there was the stick. Storm had started carrying sticks in his mouth while running. It became his way of telling Gary that everything was going right. If Storm presented Gary with the stick when they stopped, Gary knew he was being thanked for giving the team a rest. But if Gary tried to get the dogs going before they were ready, Storm refused to pick up the stick or accept it from Gary. Then Gary would know it was time for a longer rest and some food.

So strong was that line of communication—stick equaled good, no stick equaled bad—that when Storm died with a stick in his mouth, Gary knew it meant that Storm was at peace.

These, and others, were the dogs Gary trained with day after day. They were his constant companions in Minnesota and would go with him on the greatest challenge of his life: the Iditarod.

Chapter Twelve
The Iditarod

They ran the second night, and he did not sleep but his mind circled and slipped down as he rode the runners, tired but not tired. He quit thinking, quit being anything but part of the sled, part of the dogs. At one time he began to hallucinate and thought somebody was riding the sled in front of him, sitting in the basket. A blurred idea of someone.

Dogsong

Gary and the dogs were ready, waiting for their turn to be released from the chute at the Iditarod starting line. The dogs pulled and lunged, eager to be off. Gary's team was number thirty-two and the dogs had already endured watching thirty-one other teams begin. Now, at last, it was their turn.

Gary gave the command. Before hundreds of onlookers, reporters, and photographers, the anxious team of fifteen dogs pulled hard and strong—so strong that Gary couldn't control them. They ran, pell-mell, through two blocks of the city toward the first turn.

Oh, no, Gary thought as he fought to slow them. *We're not going to make the turn!*

They didn't. They rolled the sled, sending Gary tumbling to the ground in front of all those witnesses. Yet the team still pulled, Gary bouncing along behind them. At last he regained control, and together they continued through Anchorage.

After his less-than-terrific start, Gary tried to prepare himself for the obstacles that he knew would fall in his path as the race continued. He was sure all his training would pay off.

It almost wasn't enough. He had failed to take into account the fact that Minnesota is mostly flat while Alaska has not just hills, but mountains. The dogs weren't keen on traveling up and over their first mountain, but Gary managed to convince them to keep moving.

The moose proved to be a bigger challenge. On their first night—the race continues day and night without stop—the lead dog, Wilson, ran nose-first into a moose. Wilson stopped, the other dogs stopped, and Gary's sled stopped. Nothing could get them moving again.

"Now what am I going to do?" Gary said out loud when it became apparent that the moose, too, had stopped, and wasn't about to move any time soon.

"Kick the moose in the rear and get moving!" an angry voice behind him called.

Startled, Gary spun around to see another contestant

pulling to a stop behind his team. The man repeated his advice, louder this time.

With a shrug, Gary cautiously approached the moose and gave it a boot in its rear end. To his relief, the moose jumped off the trail and ambled away.

But the night wasn't over yet. Wilson took a wrong turn off the trail at one point, taking Gary and the team nearly fifty miles out of the way. To make matters worse, twenty-seven other teams, thinking Gary was on the right trail, followed them!

Gary couldn't get angry with Wilson; after all, it was Gary's job to tell the dogs where to go, so he had only himself to blame. Still, the extra miles added to his race time—and made him unpopular with the twenty-seven other teams. Gary was determined not to let that happen again. After all, he was not here just to race, but to win the race if he could.

That drive to win left him the next night, when he began having hallucinations because of sleep deprivation. The visions took many forms. His dogs seemed to run in flames. Rivers appeared where there were no rivers. An incredibly boring man with glasses and a trenchcoat sat on the sled, reading to him from a clipboard full of dull government papers. Yet the hallucinations were so real, Gary believed them: he stomped at the flames, followed the rivers, shouted at the man to shut up.

But of course they were only figments his overworked brain had created. Knowing he was hallucinating was one thing; recognizing what was real and what was illusion was something else, something Gary would fight, usually with success, for the rest of the journey.

Day after day, Gary and the dogs ran. They ran through

rocky gorges from which Gary emerged bruised and battered after losing control of the team. He slept in short spurts zipped inside his coat on the ground near the dogs. He ate chocolate chip cookies and warm bowls of moosemeat chili, and drank hot drinks provided at the checkpoints. Once, they encountered a huge buffalo and then another time, a second, less docile moose.

Then, on day six, Gary had his most powerful hallucination yet. It had started to snow, and Wilson had lost the trail. They were wandering aimlessly through the middle of Alaska, no sign of civilization in sight. Then the man appeared.

Gary had seen him once before, in Minnesota, when he was running the dogs and had taken sick deep in the woods. Then, the man had materialized and helped Gary turn the dogs toward home. And now he was back.

The man seemed to take Wilson by the collar and pull him around. The team had no choice but to follow. The man vanished once Gary was on the right track, but he reappeared each time Gary thought he might have gone wrong again. At last, Gary safely reached the checkpoint station and the man vanished for good, leaving Gary as mystified and awed as he had been that time in Minnesota.

On and on the race continued. Day ten, eleven, twelve, thirteen, through country indescribably beautiful and equally deadly to the unwary person. Two weeks went by and still the race wasn't over.

On the fifteenth day, Gary met a young Eskimo boy. The impact of that meeting stayed with him long after the race was over.

The boy, no more than a child, was lending a hand at one of the checkpoint stations. Trying to be helpful, he ran to Gary's team and grabbed Wilson's collar. Gary, greatly alarmed, jumped from the sled, certain the half-wild dogs would tear the unfamiliar boy to shreds.

"Are you crazy?" Gary shouted. "Why did you do that?"

"I want to learn about sled dogs," came the boy's surprising reply. "Will you stay at my house and tell me about them?"

Gary's fear-induced anger turned to amazement.

"*You* want to learn about sled dogs from *me?*" he said incredulously. "You live in Alaska, the home of sled dogs! I'm from Minnesota."

The boy stared at Gary. "Just because I live here, doesn't mean I know about them," he said simply.

Gary stayed with the boy's family that night, but to the boy's disappointment, Gary was too exhausted to tell him much about sled dogs. When Gary left the next morning, he still couldn't believe that the boy needed to ask him, a man from Minnesota, about running dogs.

That meeting would tug at him when the race was over, compelling him to craft his finest piece of fiction yet—a story of an Eskimo boy who teaches himself to run sled dogs.

It was two days later, day seventeen, when Gary saw Nome on the horizon. He was seventeen pounds lighter. At one point, when one of his dogs refused to eat anything but the food Gary had set aside for himself, he had survived by eating sticks of butter. His toenails were black from frostbite. He was battered, bruised, and fatigued beyond belief.

Nome grew closer and closer. At last, the race would be over and the madness of the past weeks would be over.

But suddenly, he didn't want it to end. He didn't want

to leave the beauty of the wilderness, the instinct that drove the dogs on and on, the hardships that he had endured and survived. He stopped the dogs within sight of his goal. He prepared to turn them around, to go in the opposite direction, back into the desolate tundra of Alaska. Then he heard a voice calling to him.

Another hallucination? he wondered. But the voice was familiar. It was Ruth. A friend had driven her in a jeep to the outskirts of Nome to wait for him. Her voice pulled him back to civilization. The madness, for the time being, was over.

Gary came in forty-second out of seventy-three dog sled teams, an incredible feat for someone who had never competed in the race before. When the mayor of Nome congratulated Gary on successfully completing the Iditarod, Gary just smiled and said, "I'll be back."

Chapter Thirteen
Success

"I believe in personal inspection at zero altitude. I don't think you can learn anything by listening to other people talk. You've gotta be there."

interview with Alice Evans Handy for
The Book Report, (May/June, 1991)

When Gary returned home after the Iditarod, he was a changed man. Those seventeen days had affected him profoundly. Riding a wave of emotional exaltation, he threw himself into training for the next Iditarod—and into his writing.

Writing had been a passion for fifteen years, but until the Iditarod, he hadn't had a huge success with any of his books. Now he relived his experiences in Alaska by writing about them. By delving into those recent memories, he started to dig deeper, into more distant memories, finding in them the stories that would earn him a place on every young adult reading list in the country.

One of the most powerful memories he had was of the Eskimo boy. He turned that meeting over and over in his mind, still amazed that an Eskimo boy had asked him for information about dog sledding. How could the boy have grown up in Alaska and not known about it?

Slowly, the idea for a book took shape in Gary's mind. He crafted the coming-of-age tale of an Eskimo boy who turned his back on the increasingly Western ways of his people in favor of the old ways. The boy learned these old ways from a shaman, who gave him dogs and a sled, setting the stage for a journey of survival and self-discovery. On that journey, the boy experienced much of what Gary himself had experienced during the Iditarod: the hallucinations, the gnawing hunger, the beauty and danger of the landscape, the reverence for the dogs. Gary named the boy Russel.

The words flowed from Gary's mind to the paper. Still consumed with training for his next Iditarod, Gary more or less lived with his dogs. He would run them for four hours, then stop and set up temporary camp for four hours. After feeding the dogs and himself, he would take out his notebook and write.

In 1985, the year Gary ran his second Iditarod, he published Russel's story, a novel for young readers called *Dogsong*.

Gary's previous books for children—*Mr. Tucket, Winterkill, Tiltawhirl John*, and others—had been well received, but none had been overwhelmingly successful. *Dogsong* was. Critics praised it and kids loved it. It was the latter audience that mattered most to Gary. He himself had found salvation, escape, and pleasure in books when he was growing up; he was dedicated to giving that back to his readers. His dedication was rewarded. *Dogsong* was named a Newbery Honor Book for 1985.

The Newbery Award is the highest accolade a children's book writer can receive. Though Gary hadn't been given the Award itself, the Honor was the next best thing. It proved he was a writer who had made a lasting impact. The Honor also brought him his first real financial success as a writer.

For the past two decades, Gary, Ruth, and Jim had been living in near-poverty conditions while Gary turned out one modestly successful book after another. Now, at last, they had extra money. Yet the money and celebrity status didn't matter to Gary. His days were still consumed with dogs, sleds, and writing. Always writing.

After *Dogsong* came *Sentries*, a young adult novel in four parts. It tells the coming-of-age stories of four characters, and how war intrudes on their lives. Critics were not terribly impressed with *Sentries*; they felt Gary was trying to be too clever and gimmicky, and that he had left most of his audience behind.

Gary was disappointed with the book's reception. "I was trying to show readers about war," he commented to one interviewer. "Real war, not the stuff they read about in the newspapers or see in documentaries on television. That's why I went to the veteran's hospitals and nursing homes and interviewed all those old soldiers. I wanted to get it just right." He shook his head. "But I guess they missed the point."

If Gary had been writing solely for good reviews, he might have stopped there. But he wasn't; writing for him was an obsession, one he hadn't been able to ignore since the drive to write had first captured him.

He probed his life over and over to find the experiences that would make good stories. For his next book, he decided to write a story set in the northern woods, a place he knew intimately from his childhood. In that setting, he would place a boy who had lived through a plane crash and was forced to survive with little more than a hatchet. He named the boy Brian and called the book *Hatchet*.

Step by step, Gary told how Brian learned to provide himself with food and shelter. The woods are unforgiving at first, full of biting insects and seemingly empty of food. But slowly, Brian comes to listen to the rhythm of nature around him, until one day he suddenly becomes part of that rhythm.

Gary had Brian fish as he himself had fished; hunt for the same game Gary had once hunted; sleep in a crude shelter that strong weather could tear apart, as Gary had done. Brian, like Gary, is attacked by bears, porcupines, and moose. Brian learns to start a fire by striking his precious hatchet against a rock that produces sparks. To be sure this was actually possible, Gary once spent four hours hitting a rock with a hatchet until he, too, had produced fire. Gary ate raw turtle eggs so that Brian could eat raw turtle eggs.

Gary had set out to write an exciting, danger-filled adventure story, and he had succeeded. But he wanted to give readers something else, too; he wanted them to understand that the way Brian survived was by living *with* nature, not by battling against it. It was how Gary had survived most of his life, and a lesson he felt many children would never learn because many adults didn't know it themselves.

The book struck a chord. In January of 1988, Gary Paulsen received his second Newbery Honor Award. His place as an outstanding writer for children was confirmed.

Still he continued to write, publishing three more books the next year. And then, in 1989, he published *The Winter Room*, the book that would earn him his third Newbery Honor.

Unlike *Hatchet* and *Dogsong*, *The Winter Room* is not a story of survival. In fact, Gary didn't set out to write it as a story at all, but rather as a symphony in words.

The rhythms of language, the different ways words can be joined into sentences and sentences into paragraphs, had long held a fascination for Gary. He was also passionate about choosing just the right words to capture what he was seeing in his mind's eye: the way things looked, sounded, smelled, felt, even tasted. By triggering all the readers' senses, Gary hoped to make the reading experience even more fulfilling. With *The Winter Room*, Gary achieved his goals.

The main characters, two brothers named Eldon and Wayne, live on a farm in Minnesota in the 1950s. Divided into four parts, one for each season, the book is not a chronology of seasonal events so much as an unfolding of moods, impressions, and beliefs. The delicate use of language intertwines with Gary's memories of living on farms, a perfect blend of the child he had been with the writer he had become.

All the time Gary was writing his award-winning and critically acclaimed novels, he was training with his dogs. In 1985, he went to Alaska to run the Iditarod for a second time. He didn't make it to the finish line. Caught in a violent storm, his dogs were literally blown up into the air. They were off the trail and couldn't recover. For his own safety and that of the dogs, Gary had to remove himself from the race.

His discouraging run in that Iditarod had fueled his desire to make the next race his best yet. There wouldn't be a next race, however. The breakneck pace of eighteen-hour days running dogs and writing suddenly caught up with him.

Chapter Fourteen
Weathering Changes

How could I live without the sweep of them? Without the blink on the horizon and the snap-joy of them and the reason they gave to life?

Winterdance: The Fine Madness of Running the Iditarod

Gary hurried from the check-in counter at the airport to his departure gate. He was returning from a long book-signing tour, and Logan Airport in Boston, Massachusetts, was crowded as usual. All he wanted was to get home.

Suddenly, a pain exploded in his chest, then another. The pain was so severe, his knees buckled. He fell to the floor.

"Are you okay?" A concerned woman crouched down next to him. A few other people gathered as well.

Gary grunted, then stood up slowly. He thanked the people for their trouble. "I'll be all right once I get on that flight home," he managed to say.

Someone helped him onto the plane. Gary sank down into his seat, giving the person a reassuring nod, appearing outwardly fine. Inside, however, Gary felt a coldness grip him. He wasn't sure, but he thought he had just had a heart attack. *Just let me get home,* he silently begged. *I don't want to die in Boston!*

The plane flew him to Minneapolis, where he changed to a smaller shuttle that took him closer to home. But when the second plane landed, he didn't go home. He went right to the hospital.

Ruth was with him when the doctor told him the news. "You had a severe angina attack," the physician explained. "Small arteries leading to your heart have been blocked." He went on to detail a new low-fat diet Gary was to follow. Then he said the words that almost shattered Gary.

"You'll have to give up the dogs. If you want to live, there can be no more dog sledding. Ever."

Gary thought his heart would break for real. For years, the dogs had been his constant companions. Not to have the joy of sledding was almost more than he could bear to think about. But he had no choice. As much as he loved dog sledding, he wasn't prepared to die for it. Gary sold his dogs and sleds.

Soon afterwards, Gary and Ruth decided to leave Minnesota. Without the dogs, the state didn't have as much appeal for either of them. In 1991, they packed their bags and moved with Jim to New Mexico.

This move was different from the many others Gary had had in his life. This time, there would be no twenty-five-dollar-a-month shack without electricity or indoor plumbing as there had been years before. This time, Gary and Ruth bought a ranch nestled in the mountains with acres of land surrounding it.

At the ranch, Gary tried to follow his doctor's orders. Eating a healthy diet was easy. Giving up the dogs had been difficult. Giving up eighteen-hour work days proved impossible. He had simply been working too hard for too long to shut it all down at once.

Today, Gary spends as much time as possible in front of his computer, writing. His day might start at 5:30 A.M. He takes half an hour to meditate, then has breakfast and begins writing. At noon, he'll break for lunch and answer letters. Then it's back to the computer until bedtime at midnight, only stopping to eat dinner.

Gary admits the urge to write has been stronger than ever since his heart attack. Though his heart condition appears to be under control, he can't help but feel he's racing against time. He has too much more he wants to write about to sit idle. The books pour out of him: young adult novels, adventure series, nonfiction titles for kids and adults, and picture books illustrated by his wife.

Writing isn't all Gary does, however. He also takes time to stay in touch with his most dedicated audience, children. He goes on book-signing tours, appears at book conferences, and answers the piles of fan mail he receives each week. He is featured in videos distributed by book clubs and has been interviewed on television and by newspapers and magazines across the country.

Gary continues to stay close to nature, too. He and Ruth keep horses and he enjoys going out on horseback. He goes for long walks in the woods, to nearby streams, and in the mountains. And although Gary can't run dogs anymore, he adopts dogs from the local pound to keep as pets.

Gary is never far from adventure, either. In 1994, he published *The Car*, drawing on his own experience of traveling in a car he built from a kit. In 1995, he rode his Harley-Davidson motorcycle cross-country to Alaska with a friend; the friend was perplexed to discover that Gary didn't intend to spend any time in Alaska once they got there. For Gary, the journey itself was the goal, not the destination. This escapade is recounted in *Pilgrimage on a Steel Ride*, a memoir for adults.

Sailing has long been another of Gary's passions. Years before, he and Ruth had fixed up a boat and taken it out for long treks on the Pacific. One excursion, loosely retold in his book *The Voyage of the Frog*, nearly cost them their lives—but not Gary's interest. He has sailed to Cape Horn and in the future plans to travel even farther: Australia.

With him on this journey halfway around the world will be his laptop computer, his unceasing energy, and most of all, the vivid memories of his own life. How the new memories he makes on this trip reveal themselves in his stories remains to be seen—and enjoyed.

Epilogue

Gary sat at the table, stacks of his own books beside him, waiting to sign the book for the next person in line, a gentleman in a wheelchair.

"I love your books," the man commented as Gary signed the one he held out. "They take me back to the time I could hunt. I myself spent many hours in the woods of Northern Minnesota. Thief River Falls, to be exact."

Gary looked up. Thief River Falls was the town he had grown up in. He listened as the man talked on.

"I had this great dog, a black Labrador, who used to go hunting with me. When I came home from Korea, like this," he gestured to the wheelchair, "that dog stayed by my side. He was a great comfort. I'm not sure I could have made it through the adjustment without him, to be honest."

Gary studied the man for a moment, his brain brimming with memories of the black Lab he had known in the 1950s, when the Korean War was taking place halfway around the world.

On impulse, he asked the man if he remembered the name of his dog.

The man smiled. "Remember? I'll never forget it. It was Ike." His smile faded for a moment. "I've always wondered what Ike did while I was overseas."

Now it was Gary's turn to smile. "I think I can help you out," he said. And he began to tell the man about the black Lab who had been his friend one fall so many years before.

Time Line

1939 Gary Paulsen is born on May 17 in Minneapolis, Minnesota. Oscar Paulsen leaves for Europe for World War II.

1944 Gary and Eunice move to Chicago. Gary spends the summer with his grandmother in Minnesota.

1945 Gary and Eunice travel to the Philippines to join Oscar.

1949 The Paulsens return to the United States.

1950 Gary spends the summer on his relatives' farm.

1955 Gary runs away from home and spends the summer working on a farm, then joins a carnival.

1957 Gary graduates from Thief River Falls High School.

1959 Gary flunks out of Bemidji State Teacher's College and joins the army.

1962 After being discharged from the army, Gary works for various aerospace firms.

1965 Gary walks off the job after deciding he must become a writer. He begins working at a magazine.

1966 Gary moves back to Minnesota to concentrate on writing. He publishes his first book, *Some Birds Don't Fly*.

1967 Gary moves to Taos, New Mexico.

1968 *Mr. Tucket* is published. Gary meets Ruth Wright, his future wife.

1971 Gary and Ruth marry on May 5. Son Jim is born.

1979 Gary, Ruth, and Jim move back to Minnesota.

1980 A friend gives Gary his first dog team and a beat-up sled. Gary learns how to run dogs.

1981 A moving experience in the woods with his dogs makes Gary give up trapping and hunting. He begins training for the Iditarod.

1983 Gary runs his dogs in the Iditarod.

1985 Gary races the Iditarod again, but doesn't finish due to violent weather.

1986 Gary receives Newbery Honor Award for *Dogsong*.

1988 Gary receives his second Newbery Honor Award, for *Hatchet*.

1990 Gary is diagnosed with a heart ailment and must give up running dogs. He also receives his third Newbery Honor Award, for *The Winter Room*.

1991 The Paulsens move back to New Mexico.

1993 Gary buys and begins restoring the sailboat *Felicity*.

1995 Gary rides his motorcycle cross-counry to Alaska.

1996   Gary sails his boat, *Felicity*, to Alaska.

1997   Receives American Library Association's Margaret Edwards Award for lifetime achievement.

1998   Gary sails his boat, *Ariel*, to Fiji.

Selected Books by Gary Paulsen

Mr. Tucket, 1968

Winterkill, 1976

Tiltawhirl John, 1977

The Foxman, 1978

The Night the White Deer Died, 1978

Popcorn Days and Buttermilk Nights, 1983

Dancing Carl, 1983

Tracker, 1984

Dogsong, 1985

Sentries, 1986

Hatchet, 1987

The Crossing, 1987

The Island, 1988

The Voyage of the Frog, 1989

The Winter Room, 1989

The Boy Who Owned the School, 1990

Canyons, 1990

Woodsong, 1990

The Cookcamp, 1991

The River, 1991

The Monument, 1991

The Haymeadow, 1992

The Culpepper Adventures 1–7, 1992

A Christmas Sonata, 1992

Clabbered Dirt, Sweet Grass (a book for adults), 1992

The Culpepper Adventures 8–15, 1993

Nightjohn, 1993

Eastern Sun, Winter Moon (a book for adults), 1993

Harris and Me, 1993

Dogteam, 1993

Sisters/Hermanas, 1993

The Madonna Stories, 1993

Mr. Tucket (revised edition), 1994

Winterdance, 1994

The Car, 1994

Father Water, Mother Woods, 1994

The Culpepper Adventures 16–21, 1994

The Gary Paulsen World of Adventure Series 1–2, 1994

The Tent, 1995

The Tortilla Factory/La Tortilleria, 1995

Call Me Francis Tucket, 1995

The Rifle, 1995

The Culpepper Adventures 22–27, 1995

The Gary Paulsen World of Adventure Series 3–8, 1995

Brian's Winter, 1996

Puppies, Dogs, and Blue Northers, 1996

The Culpepper Adventures 28–30, 1996

The Gary Paulsen World of Adventure Series 9–12, 1996

The Schernoff Discoveries, 1997

Sarny: A Life Remembered, 1997

Pilgrimage on a Steel Ride (a book for adults), 1997

Murphy's Trail, 1997

Tucket's Ride, 1997

My Life in Dog Years, 1998

The Transall Saga, 1998

Canoe Days, 1998

Soldier's Heart, 1998

About the Author

A graduate of Bates College, Stephanie Peters has been a children's book editor for ten years, working with such authors as Marc Brown and Matt Christopher. She is currently a freelance editor and writer.

When not at her computer, Stephanie spends her time seeing the world through the eyes of her two-year-old son, Jackson, and completing home improvement projects with her husband, Dan. An avid reader, she also enjoys hiking, combing the beach for treasures, swimming, and tennis. She and her family live in Beverly, Massachusetts.